MODERN BLACKFEET

Montanans on a Reservation

By

MALCOLM McFEE
University of Oregon

CASE STUDIES IN CULTURAL ANTHROPOLOGY

HOLT, RINEHART AND WINSTON, INC.

NEW YORK   CHICAGO   SAN FRANCISCO   ATLANTA
DALLAS   MONTREAL   TORONTO   LONDON   SYDNEY

CASE STUDIES IN
CULTURAL ANTHROPOLOGY

GENERAL EDITORS
George and Louise Spindler
STANFORD UNIVERSITY

MODERN BLACKFEET
Montanans on a Reservation

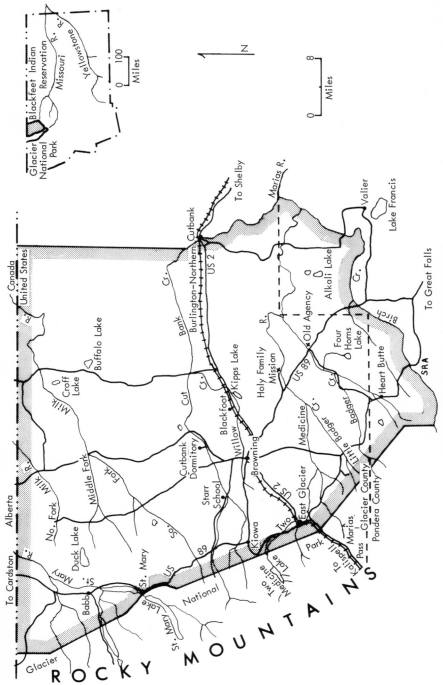

Figure 1. The Blackfeet Indian Reservation.

Foreword

About the Series

These case studies in cultural anthropology are designed to bring to students, in beginning and intermediate courses in the social sciences, insights into the richness and complexity of human life as it is lived in different ways and in different places. They are written by men and women who have lived in the societies they write about and who are professionally trained as observers and interpreters of human behavior. The authors are also teachers, and in writing their books they have kept the students who will read them foremost in their minds. It is our belief that when an understanding of ways of life very different from one's own is gained, abstractions and generalizations about social structure, cultural values, subsistence techniques, and the other universal categories of human social behavior become meaningful.

About the Author

Malcolm McFee is an Associate Professor of Anthropology at the University of Oregon where he has taught since 1965. He began his studies of the Blackfeet in 1959 while a graduate student, and has made periodic summer field trips to the reservation over the intervening years to improve his understanding of reservation life and to record the changes that have occurred through time. He received his Ph.D. degree from Stanford University in 1962, and subsequently taught at the University of Arizona before moving to Oregon. Professor McFee is presently planning to do fieldwork in Oceania to gather data that will allow a comparison of the results of U.S. and European trusteeships among Polynesian and Melanesian communities with the results of the reservation system among American Indians.

About the Book

With this case study Malcolm McFee contributes a new dimension to publications on American Indian acculturation. The results of his long term research with the Blackfeet of Montana make it clear that acculturation is not simply a linear process of assimilation or a one-way cultural adaptation to the impact of Euro-American culture. His careful analysis shows that although there are many subvarieties, there are essentially two major types of adaptation represented among the contemporary Blackfeet: the Indian-oriented and white-oriented. These represent two quite different adaptations with quite different consequences in the behavior, attitudes, and even economic standing of the two categories of people.

This book shows why policies and programs based upon simplistic assumptions of assimilation are doomed to failure. The loss of identity and total submersion in another cultural ethos is never welcomed and is usually resisted actively by people in a subordinate political and economic position. Perhaps we can see in the struggles of a substantial number of Blackfeet to retain their identity the basis for the development of a truly pluralistic cultural system. The American mania for cultural uniformity is beginning to meet with deep resistance on many fronts within our society. Whether the American cultural system is sufficiently flexible to make a pluralistic adaptation within its boundaries feasible, remains to be seen. The Blackfeet Indian case is relevant to this larger question.

Professor McFee leads us to his major conclusions through a mass of relevant information. The present Blackfeet reservation, the people who live on it, its economy, and its regional context are described. The policies of the United States government, first directed frankly at destruction of all native Indian customs and values, then at self-government, and recently threatening termination, are reviewed. The traditional culture, the echoes of which contribute qualitative uniqueness to the ways of life and self-images of the Indian-oriented Blackfeet, is summarized.

In his discussion of the Indian- and white-oriented adaptations, Professor McFee shows how people are oriented to one or the other of these cultural positions, how they interact both within and between these categories, the specific values represented in these orientations, and their status consequences. He concludes his analysis with a look into the future.

GEORGE AND LOUISE SPINDLER
General Editors

Landgut Burg, West Germany

Preface

The student of American Indian reservation life faces a dilemma: things seem to be changing rapidly; reports of local and national Indian problems proliferate, new programs continue to be initiated; yet when viewed from a longer time perspective, everything seems to remain the same. The latest Congressional studies seem to repeat many of the findings and recommendations of the Meriam Report of 1928.

I started the Blackfeet study over ten years ago with two goals in mind: to write an ethnography of the modern Blackfeet Indian reservation community and to use the data to question and refine some aspects of culture change theory. The second problem has been examined in other places (McFee 1962, 1968). This is a report of my progress toward writing the ethnography, which will, I hope, contribute to further understanding of the complexity of this and other Indian reservations.

I wrote this case study with three audiences in mind: college students, other anthropologists, and the Blackfeet. A reader from any of these groups should bear in mind the other groups to which the material is directed. A major message I want to communicate to all is that the men, women, and children who live on this Indian reservation are individuals who differ greatly in personality, aspirations, attitudes, opinions, beliefs, and behavior. They cannot be stereotyped indiscriminately as Indians or, for that matter, as Blackfeet Indians. Categorization of these people for any purpose can be done only after careful consideration of individual differences and the social and cultural contexts within which they live.

Many colleagues, teachers, and students have contributed to this study, and I can only begin to acknowledge my debt to George and Louise Spindler who as teachers and friends directed my research in the beginning years, and to my other teachers—Felix M. Keesing, Bernard J. Siegel, Bert A. Gerow, A. Kimball Romney, Alan R. Beals, and Alex Vucinich, who guided and developed my interest in anthropology.

In 1963 Morgan D. Maclachlan and Gene Reese and in 1967 Marjorie Moore, Ingrid Gram, Lynn Robbins, and Kenneth Weber worked with me on the reservation and I profited from their studies and our discussions.

I appreciate the advice of William G. Loy in the preparation of the maps and the work of Steve Anderson who drew them.

The Department of Anthropology at the University of Oregon was most supportive and I especially thank Theodore Stern, who read the manuscript and offered valuable criticism and suggestions, and Mrs. Flora Bruns and Mrs. Katherine Gill, who typed the drafts and the manuscript.

To the many people on the Blackfeet reservation to whom I pledged anonymity, I acknowledge a special debt. They gave of their time and knowledge and probably question now what I have done for them. I can only hope that they can recognize some intangible value in my attempt to portray the complexity and many facets of their life on the reservation.

To my wife, June King McFee, who shared much of the field experience, provided the unrecorded grants-in-aid, moral support, and companionship, and to my son John McFee who put up with it all, go my heartfelt thanks.

MALCOLM McFEE

Contents

1

Introduction to the Blackfeet

Blackfeet Means Many Kinds of People

THE CENTRAL THEME of this book is diversity. In some ways American Indians are different from other segments of the United States population, yet it is an oversimplification to speak of "the Indian" and "Indian problems." There are Indian problems only in the sense that it is Indians who are involved with them in Indian communities. Then, too, all Indians are not alike. Not only do tribes differ one from the other, but there is often great variation within a single tribe. The Blackfeet are not like the Hopi, neither of these is like the Kwakiutl, and all differ from the Menomini: similarly it is impossible to describe the "typical" Blackfeet Indian. Many kinds of people and diverse ways of coping with reservation life are to be found among the Blackfeet, as I will try to show.

Albert Buffalo Heart, 1878–1964, was a respected elder and honorary chief of the Piegan tribe of the Blackfeet Indians, who lived in Browning, Montana, the economic and political hub of the Blackfeet Indian Reservation. He was a tall, heavy-set, distinguished-looking man, who dressed in worn, well-laundered wool trousers and shirt, moccasins, a neckerchief, and a hat with a tall undented crown. Buffalo Heart was a poor man by the white man's standards, but to the more Indian members of the tribe he was rich in the things that counted. He had lived a long life, had learned and practiced Indian ways, and was helpful and generous to his many kinsmen and friends.

During North American Indian Days, the annual Indian encampment that is one of Browning's main summer tourist attractions, he would be one of a group of advisers who tried to insure that the ceremonies were properly Indian. If the Sun Dance ceremony was to be conducted, he would be given a principal role, as he knew some of the ritual necessary for its success. He donned his ceremonial regalia—a beaded suit of white deerskin, a Plains Indian headdress, and an air of dignity—to greet distinguished visitors and to officiate in the adoption ceremonies in which visiting dignitaries were given an Indian name and adopted, symbolically, into the Blackfeet tribe. If any family conducted a memorial service for a deceased relative, or staged a give-away to honor visitors, he was called upon to be the crier. As crier he announced the import of the ceremony, led in chanting the proper song, or cried out the occasion for the give-away and called out the names of those to be honored with a gift.

In years past he had been employed by the Great Northern Railway as an official greeter of tourists arriving by train at Glacier Park, and as an entertainer at the inns within the Park where he and his friends staged Indian dances for the tourists.

Buffalo Heart, with others of his peers, had a place on the Honorary Tribal Council, and was given a small per diem for attendance at tribal council meetings. He was often chosen to accompany council members on trips to Washington, D.C. for the purpose of lobbying for or against proposed legislation which would affect Indians. In his regalia he furnished a bit of Indian color, as well as advice, to the proceedings.

Buffalo Heart and his fellow members of the Honorary Council felt that they represented the voice of the full-blood portion of the tribe and took every occasion to make long speeches in Blackfeet, urging harmony and trust, and asking for more attention to the needs of the people. But people paid little attention to the speeches; instead they talked, moved about, and impatiently filled in time until the Honorary Councilmen had had their say. On several occasions councilmen told the interpreter: "Tell him to make it short." The people in general felt some pride in their old-timers, but mixed this with a feeling of impatience and bare tolerance when the chiefs seemed to be taking themselves too seriously.

Buffalo Heart, and the others like him, usually lived among clusters of full-bloods in the more run-down areas of town, in small outlying communities, or, in a few cases, in more remote areas of the reservation. Buffalo Heart lived in a small two-room shack on Moccasin Flat, an area of shacks and cabins without sewer or water service, on the edge of Browning. The houses immediately surrounding his were occupied by some of his kin—a married son and his family, two married daughters and their families, and the family group of his brother.

The old man's home was the center for Indian gatherings. Here he and his friends conducted the religious rituals, bundle openings, and other ceremonies they wished to celebrate. Those who were singers would gather here occasionally for a song service—a meeting where they would drum and sing old and new songs. Buffalo Heart served as a tie to the old days, a source of information on lore and ritual, and an available medicine man for those who wished an Indian cure. The younger members of his family might participate in these functions, but usually just watched with a respectful air. As one family member said: "You join in even if you don't believe—it's part of the old Indian ways."

Buffalo Heart, however, was more than a man of the past. He was a medicine man and conducted curing ceremonies, yet he and those whom he had cured more often availed themselves of the services of the local doctors and hospital. Buffalo Heart was known as a Catholic and attended church occasionally, yet he was also considered to be a repository for, and a leader in, the present-day

Browning, Montana: The administrative seat of the Blackfeet Tribe.

The drummers and part of the crowd at the North American Indian Days Celebration.

practice of the Indian religion. How did he combine or compartmentalize these two beliefs? Did he perceive the Catholic ritual as a modern means for expressing Indian beliefs? The priest, it was said, was perplexed by these questions.

There were varying perceptions of Buffalo Heart among the tribal members. Some would speak respectfully of him: "He is one of the chiefs, one of *our* people and looks after us." Others chose to praise another and saw Buffalo Heart as an old codger who had no right to the name of chief. The other chiefs might also dismiss his tales of the past and his religious knowledge as "lies." "He doesn't know anything. The truth is. . . ." So Buffalo Heart was a prophet and honored person to some, the butt of jokes to others, and, it must be noted, the judgments varied according to the situation and the person to whom the remarks were addressed. Nonetheless, this man was given a role to play, a role with limits imposed by the occasion, the time available, and by the particular people with whom he interacted.

His tie with the past was real. His father, in his youth, had hunted buffalo, fought the Cree and the Flathead, and raided the Crow camps for horses. His father had been fully conversant with Indian lore and religion, and even though a baptized Christian had remained a participant in the old culture. Buffalo Heart, himself, had lived through three-quarters of a century of radical change, a period during which new subsistence patterns were required and the problems a man was called upon to solve were concerned less and less with game and other Indians and more and more with dealing with the white man and his technology and beliefs. Buffalo Heart had tried subsistence farming, then ranching, and finally he had turned to day labor. He had seen a few Indians succeed in these endeavors,

Painted tepees: These designs are the personal property of the man who owns the tepee.

while he and the majority, due to what he believed were misfortunes beyond their control, failed. In his old age, no longer able to work, he accepted old age assistance, leased his lands to white ranchers through the local office of the Bureau of Indian Affairs, which manages lands held in trust for Indian owners, and reverted to being more fully "Indian." He admittedly did not know the old ways thoroughly. He and his friends tried to pool their knowledge, to revive the old ways and to teach these to their relatively uninterested children. He spoke of the better days of the past, which to him were the days of his father's youth. These were the buffalo days of which he had learned from the stories his father and his father's friends had told during the evenings around the fire. These days were real to him not just legend. As he saw it, Indian life in those days was not a patched up thing of half forgotten bits of knowledge which he sometimes felt life to be today.

Albert Buffalo Heart represents a small number of Blackfeet tribal members I have known and heard about, one segment of the reservation population that shares a particular status, a belief system, a mode of action, a way of life that is not limited to, nor necessarily characteristic of, old age. There are younger men and women who approximate Buffalo Heart's knowledge, beliefs, and aspirations; there are other men and women of equal relative age who share memories with the old man but who think, believe and act in another world. I will introduce a few more "representative types" to show some of the varied adaptations and adjustments made to the environment of the Blackfeet reservation. The incidents described in this section have been altered in place and detail to maintain the anonymity of the people involved, but they are based on and retain the spirit of actual events. The quoted remarks and conversations are verbatim statements made to me in situations that were similar to the contexts that have been constructed here.

I met John Arrowhead in Browning where he was waiting for the mail—a lease check was due, he said. He had just finished a fence building job and said that he hoped to find another job soon, perhaps herding sheep or "rock picking"—removing rocks and boulders that had weathered to the surface in wheat or hay fields. John is a short, wiry man, dressed in denim pants, a cowbody shirt and boots. He seldom wears a hat and nothing about his dress appears to be symbolic of the traditional Indian. Arrowhead is fifty-seven years old, had completed seven years of school, and said that he had traveled widely. His travels, usually to work in the harvesting of crops or with cattle or sheep, had taken him over a great part of the country.

During the years that I knew him, the jobs were infrequent. He is known to be a good worker, is still strong and capable, but prefers to spend more time in town, visiting and drinking with his friends. Sooner or later during our visits he would ask: "How about helping me out until my check comes? I need 50¢ to buy some gas for my friend so he can take me out home to get my clothes." I frequently gave him money and then drove around a corner to watch what happened. John would stall around for a bit, then head for the bar. Many summer days are spent standing in the shade of a building, watching the passers-by, talking with friends, and trying to get a little money for wine. He is available if a job is offered, but that seems to be a secondary consideration.

John knows much about the old religion, the societies and the Indian social activities, but he does not have the experience, status and authority to use this knowledge. He too talks of "his people," the full-blood group that once lived near each other on one part of the reservation and who still called that region home. He called the elderly man from that area "chief" and told of the important things the old man knew. Arrowhead speaks both Blackfeet and English and during conversation with me would break off in midsentence to greet a passer-by in the Blackfeet language, then resume our discussion in English. His English is adequate, but spoken with an accent and with occasional grammatical errors, usually in tense and gender, that indicate that English has been learned as a second language. He said that this was the case—he and his family spoke Blackfeet when he was growing up and his English had been learned in school.

John claims to have been a "great dancer" and a "champion" singer, but was always on the fringe of the crowd at the Indian dances and ceremonies that I witnessed. He was present, watching, often helping in some necessary but menial task, but was never in costume, never participating in dances or rituals. He knew what was going on and would describe and explain the proceedings to me. John would tell stories about the power and importance of the old ways. He believes these powers, one sensed, but he does not participate in the rituals concerning them. He does not play a significant part either in Indian social activities or in non-Indian community life. His social role remains unclear to me; he is, it seems, a bystander, one of the crowd, a man for an occasional job, but more often categorized by his acquaintances as a "good worker but a wino," a man of whom they have limited expectations.

Conversation with Arrowhead seems to confirm this view. He can not place himself. His talk is mostly of the past, of travel, work, or *past* participation in Indian dancing, singing or ceremony. He *had* been a "champion dancer . . . a good bronc rider." The highlights of his past may have become embellished by imagination. He took me on a tour of "his land" to show with pride "his cattle, his horses, his house." I knew, and he knew that I knew, that the land was his, but the house and stock belonged to another man who leased the land. In the situation of relating to a white man, at least, the need for status is more impelling than sticking to the facts.

Questions about the future draw a blank. The future lies just beyond tomorrow: "I've got a job coming up herding cattle." He evidently expects tomorrow to be like today. "I'll look for you if you come back next summer," he said, "I'll be around." He gives no clues as to further concern for what might lie ahead.

In contemplation of the past he rarely goes beyond his own experience. On occasion he vaulted back to a "Golden Age," a legendary past he and his friends accept of the trouble-free days of the Indian before the white man came. Then everybody lived well and had plenty to eat. They never became sick and lived long lives. "They didn't fight all the time either." Buffalo Heart, with all his belief in the traditional culture never went back that far. He tried to retain Indian ways of a life that his father had known; he found the better days to be those that began to disappear with the buffalo. Arrowhead holds no hope for a miraculous return of his Golden Age; Buffalo Heart, on the other hand, clung to the hope, it

Sound and a variety of sub-standard housing can be found together in some sections of Browning.

seemed, of retaining, if not regaining, some aspects of his better life. To Arrowhead, those better days are gone, part of what was lost when the white man "took everything from the Indian." The white man has become the scapegoat for all John's ills; he can do nothing about this and evidently expects no changes for the better.

John rents a small three room shack on Moccasin Flat where he lives with his wife and the younger two of their four children. His wife has made this place quite comfortable in spite of its run-down condition. John said that he also has a house on his land, where he used to live, and to which they sometimes go for a few months during the summer. Some of his friends are unmarried and live with members of their family, some have separated from their wives and have no fixed residence. Most of his close friends are equally improvident, with a life style similar to that of Arrowhead.

Why does Arrowhead not participate in the Indian ceremonies about which he knows so much? He is, he said, a Catholic, but seldom goes to church. How much does he understand of Christianity? How much does he believe in the old religion? Along with these questions, yet to be answered, are others. What factors contribute to the apparent differences between Arrowhead and Buffalo Heart? In what ways are they similar? Are the differences and similarities to be explained by age, skills, experience, education, or what? These same questions arise again and again as these men are compared with other tribal members.

I met several other older men, in ranch dress, who came to town once a week or so. One, Roy Conrad, age sixty-eight, is a farmer from the east side of the reservation who comes to town to shop, get his mail, and conduct business with the council or the agency. He and his sons farm on a small scale but he feels that they are economically independent. Roy takes an active interest in the tribal affairs, and while he has some knowledge of the past Indian culture—much of which he had learned from others in the past few years—Roy is more concerned with the recent past of the Indian, the relationships among the tribe, the agency and the tribal council. He told about the successes and failures of the various government programs and assessed the strengths and shortcomings of the various agents and superintendents who had represented the Bureau of Indian Affairs over the past forty years. He felt that the best days were those before 1934, before the Wheeler-Howard Act gave many political and economic powers to the tribe. His "Golden Age" falls in the early 1920s when a "good" agent acted as a "father" to the people and set the full-bloods to farming. "Everybody had a small ranch or farm, lived on it, and were doing all right." Since then, the council has taken over, the farm program died out, liquor has been admitted to the reservation and "ruined the young people." The full-blood has "lost out; the white man has taken over the best lands, and the whole tribe has gone down hill."

Roy is an occasional observer at the Indian Days festivities but takes no active part. He thinks that these affairs and the money spent for them are time consuming and wasteful. The people would be better off if the time and money were spent for getting themselves established on farms or ranches. Farming requires steady work with little time left over for hanging around town, dancing, drinking, and visiting.

Like Buffalo Heart and Arrowhead, Roy is a full-blood Blackfeet, and I met others who share his attitudes. Some of these are less successful economically than Roy, and are in town less frequently. Bob Sorrel Horse is one of these. He lacks the drive and, as he lamented, the capital with which to realize the "dream" he has of building a small ranch. "I think a lot when I'm alone. I have this dream to get some money and fix this place up right—a nice house and a good place. First I'd get electricity in to pump the water. I had planned to remodel the house—my father built this a long time ago—to have a place I'm not ashamed of." The dream has not been realized, but I was impressed by the order he maintains around his log cabin and by the effort that has gone into the utilization of the little Bob has.

Because these men are seldom in town, I did not get to know them well enough to assess their cultural backgrounds, but did gather that they had had the opportunity, in their families and during their childhood and youth, to learn aspects of the traditional Blackfeet culture. They speak Blackfeet as well as good English. The Indian accent, which I can only describe as a rather musical variation in pitch and a fairly explosive phrasing, neither of which conforms to general English speech patterns, but which are more familiar to the speaker of Blackfeet, is slightly noticeable. These men appear to have lived within this more traditional cultural context without having absorbed much of it, and at the same time have striven toward goals of economic success more related to those of western culture. They feel no need to reaffirm, exaggerate, or separate an Indian part of their lives as opposed to a white part. They are Indians. They can be antiwhite in matters concerning the tribe and the reservation, but see their future in terms of work, money, and building capital—the ranch, the farm, the herd. Some people represented by Roy and Bob achieve more success than others in this endeavor.

I also met some younger men, in appearance and dress youthful counterparts of John Arrowhead. They, however, spend less time standing around, seem to be more animated in their conversation, and move more often at a somewhat quicker pace. Like Roy and Bob, these men are not in town regularly. Joseph Renault, for example, is seen for a few days and then is gone for weeks at a time. He appears to differ in a number of ways from the others I have talked about.

Upon acquaintance, I found that this man is an active seeker of work, is known to be a good worker who is called whenever jobs are available. He also leaves the reservation to look for work in the harvests, to fight forest fires, or to take construction jobs. His employment is irregular and seasonal, yet he takes advantage of all such work available.

Joe is thirty-two years old, ⅝ Blackfeet, married but separated from his wife. When home, on Badger Creek near Old Agency, he lives with his mother, a sister, her two children, and two of his children that his mother is raising. These seven people live in a two room frame house that is badly in need of repair.

Joe knows something of Indian practices and has participated occasionally in social dancing. He speaks English quite fluently and claims to know very little of the Blackfeet language. He talked of both work conditions and old Indian ways during our discussions, but as a participant in the work realm and as one who was marginal to the Indian ways. He is a Catholic by faith, but here, too, is seldom a participant. I met him in town, where he frequently comes "between jobs" to meet his friends, have a few drinks and then, when his cash is gone, leave to find more work.

Because the opportunities to get better acquainted with Joe were few, I have but a shallow impression of his way of life. He impressed me as a man who, if trained, could become a steady worker, or who might just as readily fall into a pattern of life like that of Arrowhead as jobs become harder to find as he grows older. I learned little of his values or the beliefs to which he is committed; his goals, at least as he expressed them, seem to be limited to the next job and the spending of the money he earns. He talked occasionally of going on relocation, or of signing up for on-the-job training, but hinted that these thoughts have been with him for several years and have never gone beyond the inquiry stage. He had been in the Army for two years where he had learned welding, but found no demand for that trade on the reservation. "I may go to Denver and get a welding job," he said once, but he never went and I felt that in all probability he never would. If, in later years, he should go, and is successful in finding a trade and sticking to it, he might avoid the Arrowhead pattern. Yet he gives the impression that he would expect to fail and would return to the reservation. What creates these impressions of a man who at first seems so open and self-assured? The assurance is there when he talks of the present, but when he is led into thinking about the future he give the impression that this is unexplored territory. He has only vague ideas to work with. Also, he seems to have but shallow ties with the past, limited to his own experience plus what little he knows of his parents' life. Perhaps he is yet too young to be concerned with the past; but why no thought of the future? Again a question for further reflection.

I met some younger men, visibly Indian, who also were raised in the more traditional full-blood homes, but who are better educated than others from a similar background. They speak both languages fluently and are able interpreters. Raymond Black Plume expressed a primary goal of these men. "I want to make a life by combining what is best of the Indian way with the best from the white way." These men see themselves as representatives of the full-blood group within the council, and actively seek office. Raymond has served several terms.

He participates in Indian ceremonies and knows much of the old religion and rituals, although he himself is a Christian and an active church member. His commitment to the old beliefs is difficult to assess. Although he is more than tolerant of the old practices, and gives the impression of being a respectful non-believer, occasional statements lead me to believe that there is much in the old religion that appeals to him, and he may have assimilated some of this into his Christian practice. Raymond's father, recently dead, had been one of the "chiefs," so Raymond's knowledge of Blackfeet lore and life came directly to him in his childhood home. Beyond this, he has traveled widely and has studied and accepted much white culture from his schooling.

I met a few others like him, all of whom are interested in tribal affairs, and work regularly in council or agency jobs, or as clerks, teachers or tradesmen. These people, while differing as individuals, represent another kind of full-blood Indian.

Raymond, age forty-one, is married and has four children. His frame house has four rooms and, differing from those mentioned earlier, has more furnishings, including a refrigerator and a television set. He has a recent model automobile that is kept in good condition, but shows little attention to minor details of upkeep.

The house is located near those of other members of his family along a small creek, several miles from Browning, where the family members pooled their labor to develop a stock ranch. When Raymond is serving on the council, or employed at a council or agency job, he can count on his brothers, uncles, and nephews to look after the place, while his income, which is large in terms of the reservation average, will be used to keep all the family going when they need money.

These activities also indicated that Raymond is keenly interested in the present, ongoing activities of tribe and ranch. He also likes to talk of the past—a past in which he is interested and of which he has heard much from his father. However, he has no desire to return to those days, only a wish to use what good the old culture has to offer for today. He also thinks much about the future. He has goals for the people and for himself. He intends to build up the ranch until it can support the family. "I'll be ready if termination[1] comes," he said; "I'll be able to take care of myself and family." His progress toward this end appears to be slow, but he is making headway.

Raymond said that his greatest problems arise from the jealousy of his

---

[1] Termination of the Bureau of Indian Affairs and the special relationships between Indians and the federal government.

friends and neighbors. The people like to see one of their boys get ahead but at the same time are jealous of his success. Consequently he is often the subject of gossip. People like Arrowhead praise him at one time, while at other times they lump him with the "crooks" on the council who see to it that all the benefits go to members of their own families but do nothing for the other people. He is criticized by Sorrel Horse for the conveniences to be found in his home. "Just go call on one of those councilmen. He'll have everything in his house, a radio, TV, a refrigerator, and probably will even have beer in it. He'll tell you that he's worked hard for it. But he hasn't. He tries to live like a white man while we have nothing." Such criticism and gossip soon led me to believe that even the full-blood Blackfeet do not see eye to eye on many things. They differ as to what they want in life, how to get these things, and in their ability to achieve them. Raymond said that there is conflict also between the full-bloods and the mixed-bloods. The latter, who make up roughly three-fourths of the tribal population, are more progressive, according to Raymond. "They try to push things the old folks don't understand. It isn't a caste division, just a mistrust of method and plan."

Many other people I met varied in family backgrounds, in jobs, or in personal appearance from those already discussed, but there were certain basic similarities in attitudes toward themselves and others, similarities of comprehension of, and interest in, Indian ways versus white ways. These characteristics make one person more like Arrowhead, another more like Raymond Black Plume, and yet another more like Joe Renault. There are many others, however, who seem to represent variations of a contrasting way of life.

Carl Hunter, thirty-seven years of age, is ⅝ Blackfeet and the son of mixed-blood parents. He had completed the eighth grade and served two years in the army, eight months of which was in active combat in Korea. His wife is ½ Blackfeet, and they have five children.

Carl owns no land or home of his own. He and his family live with his father, a widower who owns a two-room log cabin built in 1939 under one of the reservation housing programs. This is one of several houses clustered along Blacktail Creek from which the daily water supply is drawn. The home is sparsely furnished. The wood range serves for both cooking and heating. A wooden table and kitchen chairs provide dining and seating facilities. A cot, two double beds, and a crib complete the furnishings. The limited space and the sleeping requirements for eight people allow for little more.

Carl is employed regularly during the time of year (seven months) when work is available. He has worked on the railroad section crew and as a ranch hand, but considers construction labor to be his main occupation. His income is not high, but is steady and sufficient to qualify him for unemployment benefits. His father has land which is leased for grazing and receives a small pension for his years of service as a janitor and caretaker for the Bureau of Indian Affairs. This money, pooled with Carl's income, usually carries the family through the winter. Only occasionally is it necessary for the family to apply for welfare assistance.

According to Carl, neither he nor his father have any knowledge of the traditional Blackfeet culture. All of the family have been raised as Catholics. Both his father and mother had attended the Catholic boarding school and stayed to work there for several years—his father as a caretaker and his mother as a cook.

Carl attended the small public school near his childhood home followed by a few months at Browning High School. He dropped out because there was no bus service from his home to town at that time and it was hard to find a place to live in Browning. No one in his family can speak Blackfeet. He takes no interest in the more Indian social events, such as dancing, encampments, and stick games; his recreational activities center around card games and visiting with his family and neighbors along the creek during the winter. During the rest of the year he spends most of his spare time hunting. A few evenings are spent with his brother and a few friends in town, where they get a bottle and drive around in a car, stopping now and then for a few drinks. They usually end up at a friend's house where they play cards and "hang one on."

Carl, like some of the others, also seems to live in the present and think little about the future. He talks easily of the past, but with an air of detachment that puzzles me. He can relate a series of troubles and tragedies almost as if these things had happened to someone else. Is he a stoic, or is he carefully guarding his emotions from a stranger? His life conditions are extremely barren and harsh compared with mine. How can he appear so happy and satisfied with things as they are? Is it because he has neither known nor expects to know any other way? Yet he has had opportunities both on and off the reservation and in the army to meet others who live differently.

To probe into these questions, I asked about job opportunities on and off the reservation. What do the tribe and the bureau do to help people find work? "They are trying to attract industry to the reservation," he replied, "and are building programs for relocation and on-the-job training. None of these has produced much yet." His reply when asked whether or not he has considered relocation was that he had thought about it but never applied. "I don't have much trouble getting a job. Some of the fellows have gone on relocation and done all right. Others didn't like it and came home." The answers imply that he is doing well enough at seasonal work. There was no expression of dissatisfaction with his own subsistence pattern.

By my standards, eight people in two rooms is overcrowded, so I asked if there was any provision by either the tribe or the bureau to help a man if he wants to add onto or repair his home. "Yes, they have a setup for that," was the answer. "I guess we could get a loan like that if we needed it." This again seems an expression of satisfaction with the way things are. He recognizes no need for either more room or for repairs.

Carl has nothing to offer when asked about his future plans. I inferred that he would continue as he is. What culture pattern does he reflect—Indian or white? Or is his outlook a clue to a new subculture that has developed under reservation conditions? Is this a way of life related not so much to the reservation as to a more general American subcultural pattern that develops under conditions of deprivation, a way displayed here by a man who happens to be part Indian and who lives on an Indian reservation? This question will require further examination.

Robert Thompson was in town to get parts for a mower. His ranch is north of town and the prairie grass was about ready to be cut for hay. Robert appears to be about twenty-six years old, said he is married and has two children. He is ⅛

Blackfeet and his wife is $\frac{1}{16}$. He was dressed in the familiar blue denim pants, cowboy shirt, boots, and hat.

The ranch Robert operates belonged to his father who had established the home and herd in 1940. Robert had been given a few cows while he was in school as payment for his work on the ranch. As his father grew older, more and more of the work had been turned over to Robert and his brother, until they have assumed complete charge. His father is dead; his mother lives with him.

What is Indian about Robert? He said he does not speak the language, although his father could. He knows nothing about the old Indian religion, lore, or medicine. He and his parents before him were raised as Catholics and attended church regularly. His great-grandmother was a full-blood Blackfeet, but his father and grandfather had both married white women, so he felt that his home background and training had been no different than it would have been if he had had no Indian ancestors, and had been born and raised on a similar ranch across the reservation line. Because they have lived on the reservation, he and members of his family have picked up, by observation and hearsay, a superficial knowledge of Indians and Indian ways, but he evinced little interest in these things. A few of his relatives have taken an interest in the more formal aspects of pan-Indianism; they participate, for example, in the major Indian Pow Wows such as the annual Indian Encampment at Sheridan, Wyoming. Their participation is limited to marching or riding in the parade, entering a daughter in the Miss American Indian contest, or acting as a judge for this and other contests. They neither camp in the tepee circle nor participate in the dances.

Robert has gone to school with people who are more Indian than he, so he knows many kinds of people. His social activities, however, have been limited to his family and their close friends—people much like himself. He casts Indian problems into one or the other of two contexts. His immediate response to a question about Indians is to talk about reservation problems, of land, leasing, cattle, employment, and of the conflicts between "Indians" (the reservation population) and the "whites" (government officials, white farmers who bought or leased Indian land, and the local merchants). Within this context he is aligned with the tribe and the Indians. When the discussion turns to matters of Indian culture, his focus changes. At times he felt that people should let the Indians live the way they want to. At other times he commented that these beliefs and practices are doomed to extinction and should be helped on their way. The impressive thing was that this does not concern him. He suggested that I call upon some of the "Indians." "They can tell you about this." Within this context, Robert did not see himself as an Indian. What is an Indian? When and under what circumstances do people of mixed-blood see themselves as Indians and when not? Does the full-blood Indian think of people like Robert as Indian or white? Are they considered to be Indian or non-Indian by the white people who live around them?

Robert's recreational activities center around the ranch life. He rarely attends the local Indian Days festivities. He is, however, among the audience at all local rodeos, fairs, and school meetings, and takes part in a few community service projects—those concerned with community development, schools, youth programs, cattle and range management programs.

An urban home, Browning.

It is difficult to find anything Indian about Robert Thompson. He neither looks nor acts like an Indian. He knows nothing of Indian ways, and does not consider himself to be an Indian except in the limited context already mentioned. He is, nonetheless, a member of the tribe and a resident of the reservation.

There are other people who are noticeable because they dress more like city people than like country people and tend to live in the larger and more expensive homes on the reservation. One of these is Henry Rogers.

Henry is forty-five years of age, his wife is white and they have two children of junior high school age. He shares many of the traits of people like Robert Thompson, but has a distinctive life style that sets him apart. Except when hunting or fishing he dresses in sports clothes or business suits. He is urbane and sophisticated. Henry knows more than most of the people about history, literature, and the world of business and politics. He has kept abreast of world-wide current events. After two years of college, Henry served in the Air Force as a master sergeant, and he has traveled extensively around the United States. Unlike John Arrowhead, Henry's travel was not as an itinerant laborer, but as a tourist and sight-seer, a visitor of historical sites, museums, night clubs, and other tourist attractions. He lacks Robert Thompson's interest in rodeos and the first hand contacts with ranch life. His interests are in business and politics at both the tribal and national levels.

He and his brother had inherited land, and rather than lease it for grazing as so many others do, they have contracted pasturage to outside cattlemen, that is, they "run cattle." This means providing range and care for outside herds during the grazing season at a set price per head "run" on their land. This is a method of land exploitation, according to Henry, that for a little management and expense yields up to ten times the income that can be gained from the usual grazing lease contracts. Henry lives more by brains than brawn. Such an operation leaves him free for other ventures—to serve on the council, to hold an agency job, to promote a new venture for the tribe, or to work on a new business deal of his own. Henry is an administrator, a promoter, an entrepreneur.

Henry owns one of the better homes in Browning. The house is well maintained, the large lawn is mowed regularly. Shade trees, shrubs and flowers are numerous. The house is well furnished with overstuffed furniture, a coffee table, bookcases, television, radio, a hi-fi set, refrigerator, freezer, electric stove, and central heat—all the comforts of middle-class city dweller's home. Each of these things, by itself, would not set Henry apart from his fellow tribal members. Other people have well-maintained houses; other have lawns, trees and flowers. Many have new cars like Henry's. It is the total combination of these things, coupled with his sophistication and more widely ranging interests and economic operations, that differentiates Henry from the others.

As I got to know Henry better, I became aware of certain values, drives, and attitudes that were unlike those of the other people I have described. Henry is interested in the old Indian culture, but his knowledge of this has been acquired intellectually, through books and studied observation. He is ¼ Indian but has had nothing of Indian life transmitted to him through his home environment, childhood training, or other experience: He remained apart from the Indian behavior expressed by friends and schoolmates during the years he had attended a small country school. In the Browning High School he mixed with people more like himself. He was then among the "more Indian" of the pupils but does not appear to have recognized the things that made them different from him and his friends. The segregation between his friends and others had not been a conscious act. It just "came about." He went away to college and found work in Great Falls after dropping out. Following this came World War II and his years in the service, after which he settled in San Francisco for a year.

Henry returned home to help his brother set up a program for the use of the family lands and while doing this became involved in the problems of Indian land management. At this time he became aware of the plight of the large majority of the reservation residents. He had found a new goal for himself. He bought his house and stayed in Browning to pursue his interest in Indian affairs and to try to better the conditions of the Indian people. Neither he nor I could separate the motives that spurred this interest. He is genuinely involved in this cause and at the same time the cause offers an opportunity for personal achievement—in politics, in tribal affairs, and in economic ventures. It suffices that Henry has found a goal toward which he can apply his particular interests, abilities, and drives.

In this work he often finds himself teamed with Raymond Black Plume, and it was by contrasting these two men and their approach to and understanding of the problems of the Indian that I became aware of other characteristics of Henry Rogers. Both men have a genetic tie back into the traditional Blackfeet culture. Raymond, however, has learned what he knows of it by growing up with it; Henry has learned of it by study in later life. Raymond grew up under conditions that exposed him to two sets of traditions, ideals, goals, attitudes, and beliefs. He has had to select and adjust, to reconcile and accommodate, to give and take from what he encounters as he formulates his goals and adopts means to achieve them. Henry, on the other hand, has been socialized to the white pattern. His new dedication to the solution of Indian problems has awakened an interest in Indian traditions. He learns what he can of Indian ways, but has no need to internalize these, or to accommodate to them in his everyday life. Raymond's goal is to make a life by combining what he finds to be the best of both the white and Indian traditions. Henry, whether he realizes it or not, works toward changing the Indian to greater acceptance of white ways. He would retain the symbols and ritual of "being an Indian," but spoke of providing steady work and better education as the bases of change. If these could be gained, he believes, the people would correct other deficiencies. Raymond, on the other hand, emphasizes better housing and improving sanitation first, then jobs and education. To Henry, better homes and sanitation would follow from more jobs and education. Raymond supports the preservation of Indian ways because they have a meaning for him—they are a part of his identity. Henry supports these same things because he feels that the Indian children need the knowledge of their cultural heritage as a psychological support for their feelings of self-worth as they learn to live in the modern world—they need to know that they are not just the "descendants of heathen savages." He wants to set up formal elective courses in the schools to teach Blackfeet history and culture. Raymond, in the meantime, teaches these things to his children and their friends as a part of their childhood training, by story and example. One man is involved objectively and rationally; the other, more subjectively and emotionally.

Henry, because of his experience, has different values and attitudes that have not been changed by intellectual understanding of Indian problems. Two incidents I observed seem to support this. Once during a discussion of housing conditions on Moccasin Flat, Henry expressed the wish that he could get the council to make an appropriation to buy grass and flower seed to give to all the householders in that area. If the council would do this and encourage the people to plant the seeds, he thought, it would make quite a difference in the appearance of the neighborhood and should help get the people interested in the improvement of their homes and yards. I do not think that Raymond would support such a plan. He has neither lawn nor garden; other problems are more pressing in his eyes, other needs more important.

The second incident occurred at a public gathering that I attended with Henry and some of his relatives. A small full-blood boy came up to play with Henry's six-year-old niece. The two children chattered away together, but their play was halted when it began to involve physical contact. A slightly older niece broke up the play remarking: "You can't let those full-blood children touch you. They are dirty and have germs." This reveals a difference in attitudes toward cleanliness and health that reflects a social distance between some members of the reservation population. These are differences in attitudes based on dissimilar backgrounds and experience and in no way raise a question about the sincerity of Henry's concern about Indian welfare. He sees things from one perspective, a viewpoint that might be shared with some of the men I have described, but undoubtedly at odds with the point of view of Buffalo Heart, Arrowhead and Black Plume.

I have shown some of the kinds of people I met on the Blackfeet reservation. Even when allowance is made for individual differences, these people vary considerably in experience and life styles. Several questions were posed above about these men and their modes of adaptation and adjustment to reservation life. These and similar questions guided my fieldwork. The things I learned, the data I gathered, analyzed and reported in detail elsewhere (McFee 1962), provided the foundation and support for what follows.

Fieldwork

The fieldwork for this study was done during the summers of 1959 and 1960 and as I returned to the reservation in 1963, 1967, and 1970 to increase my understanding of these people and to observe the developments in their lives over time. I began my study with the assumption that there were many kinds of people on the Blackfeet Reservation and my fieldwork procedures and data gathering methods were aimed at uncovering and demonstrating the greatest variety possible.

Field techniques included observation, sometimes as a participant in some activity, and both formal and informal interviewing. I was known to be an anthropologist interested in studying the way of life of the people on the reservation, and in this role was accepted as an observer at all public functions. It was a pleasure to accept all invitations into homes, to private parties or other gatherings. In some situations notes could be taken freely—the notebook was recognized as part of my anthropological equipment. In other situations where note taking did not seem proper, or where my role was unknown to most of the people present, no notes were taken. In such cases the conversations and activities were written up as soon as possible after the event.

During the spring and summer of 1960 I tried a sampling procedure to help insure that I was meeting a random collection of people and to further my aim of finding variety. Observation and informal methods were continued, but a major effort was put into collecting data by formal interviews, using a questionnaire with the members of a random sample of adult men in order to get comparable data from a wide range of people. Less formal methods were continued during the subsequent visits.

Guides, interpreters, or other helpers were seldom used because often the man selected for this purpose was disliked by an informant and became more of a hindrance than a help. In most cases where I was working with men in the sample, I asked for directions to where the man lived, went there, introduced myself, explained my purpose as clearly as I could and then asked the man to work through the questionnaire with me. Each was assured that his anonymity would be protected, and names were not appended to the interview notes.[2] No one refused to be interviewed. Some gave less information than others and some were more willing than others to answer questions, but all men contacted gave some answers to my questions. I encouraged people to talk at length about the questions and this, as well as the great distances I had to travel to find a specific individual

---

[2] Fictitious names are used throughout the book, except in quotations from public sources.

and the frequent necessity of making more than one trip, limited the number of interviews achieved.

The result was a set of minimum basic answers to the questionnaire from the carefully controlled sample of thirty-three men, plus a large body of additional information from most of them, usually about their experiences, family backgrounds, attitudes, goals, and values. A generally similar body of data was recorded by the less formal methods from forty-five other people, men and women. These data were expanded by observation of daily life—the context within which people did or did not do the things they said they did, agreed or disagreed vocally or visibly with each other's statements.

Other sources of information were used. Permission was obtained to examine the minutes of the tribal council meetings. Records and documents held by the tribe and agency were made available on request, and the archives of the Museum of the Plains Indian, at Browning, was a valuable source of information. In addition, tribal and Bureau of Indian Affairs officials, museum personnel, school administrators, clergymen, businessmen, and citizens gave willingly of their time to answer questions. I am still amazed and pleased at how many people were willing to put themselves out to help my study, to talk with me, and to explain their point of view, when there was no reason beyond civility for them to do so.

All these sources of information served as cross checks on the reliability of the data. The information received from one person was checked for accuracy by questions put to other people, and by comparing answers from other sources, one against the other. Lack of agreement among respondents need not be interpreted always that one was right and the other wrong—they simply disagreed. Also, much of the information could be checked out by observation. I was there and could often compare reported events with actual events, reported behavior with actual behavior. Such cross checking uncovered two cases where the answers to my questionnaire were shown to be so questionable that the data could not be used.

In Prospect

In the rest of the book I shall examine further the variations in the lives of the Blackfeet people, the social groupings that appear to be present, and the cultural characteristics of these groupings, and I shall try to explain how these came about. Toward these ends the reservation and its people are described in relation to the state and nation. The purpose of the next chapter is to note the many things the Blackfeet share with the rest of the nation, and to identify the ways in which they, as a whole, are distinguished from their non-Indian neighbors. The roots of these differences lie in the Indian heritage, described in Chapter 3, and in the history of culture change since the beginning of their white man problems, reviewed in Chapter 4. In following chapters I shall examine in more detail the social and cultural variation within the tribe that I introduced in this chapter, and shall review in the Epilogue the kinds of things that might have happened to Albert Buffalo Heart and the others between 1959 and 1970.

2

The Blackfeet Reservation
and Its People

Introduction

T HE BLACKFEET INDIAN RESERVATION, as a geographical region with definable borders, can be described by the usual environmental concepts. The people who live there, however, cannot be treated so simply, because the population is greater than the membership of the Blackfeet tribe for whom the reservation was established. Both whites (about 3,500) and Indians (about 6,400) live here, and among the latter are found both members of the tribe (about 6,200 of the 10,000 plus tribal enrollment) and nonmembers (about 200).[3] Yet all share many political economic and sociocultural activities that make up the general way of life of this region, the counties within which the reservation lies, the state of Montana, and the United States of America.

This is an American community and it exhibits many of the social and cultural dimensions of such a community. But it differs because it is located on an Indian reservation and the bulk of the population is Indian. These people are Indians in addition to being citizens of the United States, Montana, county and town.

For this reason the discussion is presented in two parts: (1) a description of the geographic, economic, political and social dimensions that are shared by the greatest number of the people of the region; and (2) an examination of the unique and particular cast given to these dimensions because this is a reservation

---

[3] These and other population figures to follow are estimates based on figures from a variety of sources. Each source, the Census Bureau, the Bureau of Indian Affairs, and the Blackfeet tribe define the population differently. The tribe is concerned with tribal members; the B.I.A. with all Indians on the reservation of ¼ or more Indian descent for some purposes, or with only those Indians who hold trust lands in other cases, which means only Blackfeet but not all Blackfeet Indians. The U.S. Census figures probably include all persons who claim to be Indians, Blackfeet or other, yet may not include, by this definition, some persons who are on the tribal rolls. Land use and other economic figures, too, often differ because the information is reported in common categories, but these categories are given differing definitions.

Reservation grazing lands.

for Indians. This provides a summary of the environmental, social and cultural characteristics shared by *all tribal members* who reside on the reservation which will serve as a context for an examination of intratribal differences.

The Regional Habitat

The Blackfeet Indian Reservation, approximately 2,400 square miles in area, is located along the eastern slopes of the Rocky Mountains in northwestern Montana. It is bounded on the north by the United States-Canadian international boundary, on the west by the foothills of the Rockies, on the south by Birch Creek, and on the east by a line commencing at the junction of Cut Bank Creek and the Marias River, extended northward following the center of Cut Bank Creek for twenty miles, and then directly north to the Canadian border (see Fig. 1, frontispiece map).[4]

The land within these boundaries consists mainly of high, rolling prairies which are interrupted by numerous rivers and creeks, and occasional ponds, lakes, buttes, and hills. A narrow strip, three to ten miles wide and about sixty miles in length, along the western border includes a few barren peaks of the Rocky Mountains and the forested hills and valleys of the foothill region. The mountains reach heights of eight to ten thousand feet, but the greater portion of the reservation ranges in altitude between forty-five hundred feet in the west to thirty-five hundred feet above sea level in the east.

---

[4] The northern boundary was established by the Treaty of 1855 (U.S. Statutes XI, 1859:657), the western by the sale of the mountain portion east of the Continental Divide by an agreement ratified by Congress in 1896 (U.S. Statutes XXIX, 1897:353). The southern boundary was established by an act of Congress in 1874 (U.S. Statutes XVIII, 1875:28), and the present eastern border was set by an agreement of sale between the Blackfeet and the United States, ratified by Congress in 1888 (U.S. Statutes XXV, 1889:113).

This is predominantly short-grass prairie country. The hills are covered in late spring and summer by highly nutritious native grasses which can be mowed for hay in early fall. The uncut grasses and the stubble become dry by fall, yet they retain their nutrients and provide good grazing throughout the better part of the winter (Burlingame 1942:268, *Montana Almanac* 1957:74).

Trees are confined mostly to the immediate foothills of the Rockies where both evergreen and deciduous growth is quite dense, and to the river beds and valleys where cottonwoods and willows predominate.

The reservation and the nearby mountains support an abundant wildlife population, including birds, fish, game animals—for example, bear, deer, antelope, elk, mountain goat, and sheep—and fur bearers, such as beaver, mink, badger, muskrat, and skunk.

Hunting and fishing of game varieties is controlled on public, federal, and tribal lands by state, federal, and tribal authorities. The Indians are not subject to these regulations on the reservation and hunting and fishing provide an important supplement to the diet of many families. Some men trap for furs as either a regular or supplementary source of income, but the game population, while numerous, is not sufficient to provide subsistence for more than a few.

The climate varies with the relative distance from the mountains, but the plains part of the reservation can be characterized as a region of low precipitation and low humidity. Most of the moisture falls during the months from May to September, with lesser amounts, in the form of snow, sleet and rain, falling during the winter for an average annual total of about fourteen inches.

Lower Two Medicine Lake at dusk.

Winters are long and cold, summers short and hot. Extreme temperature changes, up to 40 degrees, occur frequently during any season and within any twenty-four hour period. Winter temperatures, from November through March, average 24 degrees Fahrenheit but may go as low as 50 degrees below zero, while frequent chinook winds often raise the temperature to 50 degrees above and rapidly melt any accumulated snow. Summer temperatures range into the 100's but again, rapid fluctuations accompany sudden storms. The earliest frosts are apt to occur in September and the latest in May, giving an average of 100 to 102 frost free days annually. The area is subject to persistent westerly winds, which can attain velocities to seventy-five miles per hour.

All in all this is a region of definite and intense weather, be it hot, cold, wet, dry, calm, or windy. A man can either lean into the wind or go with it, either seek protection from the cold and heat or endure these when necessary. The climate is an environmental phenomenon that requires active accommodation.

Regional Population and Economy

The reservation includes portions of two counties. Approximately 70 percent of Glacier county's 2,974 square mile area and perhaps 40 to 45 percent of its about 12,000 population are included within reservation boundaries. The southern portion of the reservation incorporates approximately 17 percent of Pondera county's 1,643 square mile area and about 7 percent of its estimated 7,800 population. Major concentrations of people in the area are in its small towns, the largest of which is Cut Bank, the Glacier county seat, with a population nearing 5,000 persons, followed by Browning with an estimated 2,400, East Glacier near the western reservation line with perhaps 350, and Valier, the county seat of Pondera, with about 750 persons. Other towns and hamlets will be introduced later.

The main line of the Burlington-Northern Railroad (formerly the Great Northern Railway) from Chicago to the Pacific coast transverses the Blackfeet reservation, and major east-west U.S. Route 2, parallels the railroad. Both connect Browning, the major trade center on the reservation, with cities to the east and west. U.S. Route 89 runs through the reservation from north to south, connecting Browning with Canadian highways to Banff and Calgary to the north and providing rapid access to Great Falls, Montana, 125 miles to the southeast.

An airport at Cut Bank, 36 miles east of Browning and just across the reservation border, and landing strips on the reservation, at Starr School and Babb, are available to private and nonscheduled aircraft, and an additional air strip is planned for East Glacier. Scheduled airline service is available at Kalispel, 100 miles to the west, and at Great Falls.

Telephone, telegraph, radio and television provide ties into the network of national communication. Television comes in from Great Falls and from a Canadian station at Lethbridge, Alberta. Radio stations in both nearby towns and distant cities provide a variety of programs. *The Great Falls Tribune,* a daily, and weekly publications of *The Cut Bank Pioneer Press* and Browning's *Glacier Reporter,* provide newspaper coverage for reservation readers.

Ranching and farming are the major economic pursuits of the people of these counties. The northern and western portions contain excellent natural grazing areas and are extensively used by both residents and outsiders for grazing of beef cattle, sheep, and horses. The eastern third of Glacier county and the greater portion of Pondera are subject to lesser amounts of rainfall than the more westerly portions but have more frost free days, and have been utilized to a greater extent for both dry and irrigation farming. Principal crops are wheat, barley, and hay.

Oil and natural gas production and refining are important industries, with the principal producing fields lying just to the east of the reservation limits. Producing wells on the reservation in both the northeast and southeast corners may be tapping these same fields. Oil is also being pumped in the northwest part of the reservation and there has been revived interest recently in exploring the potential of the western foothill strip. Oil lease money and bonus payments for leasing rights have provided a fluctuating but important prop to the local economy. There has been little manufacturing or lumbering, although the foothill strip, adjoining national forests and Glacier Park, has a lumber potential that is slowly being realized as the tribal mill in Browning increases its lumber output and new wood products industries are being attracted to the reservation.

The population, with an economic base of beef, wool, grain, and hay, also supports businesses, services, schools, churches, and government. Banking and financing institutions are available in Cut-Bank, Browning, Conrad and Valier. Dependent children, and also those who are needy, aged, blind, or disabled are provided for by the county public welfare system established by state law and financed by tribal, county, state, and federal funds.

Like the other people of Glacier and Pondera counties the tribal members are citizens of the United States and of the state of Montana. They participate in national and state politics and in the county, precinct, school district, and town governments according to their places of residence. Reservation boundaries, it will be seen, create an added dimension. They overlie the county system but do not obliterate, change, or directly affect it. Democrats, Republicans, independents, and disinterested voters play their respective parts at all levels of politics.

The reservation region is served by the Montana State Public Schools system. County school districts, with one or two exceptions, cross reservation lines. The public schools that have Indian pupils receive federal support under the Federal Impact Area Act (PL 874) (U.S. Statutes LXIV, 1, 1950:1100) and the Johnson-O'Malley Act of 1934 (U.S. Statutes XLVIII, 1934:596) which in differing ways provide for payments to public schools in lieu of the taxes not received from Indian lands held in trust. Elementary schools, varying greatly in size, plant, and staff, are found in all settled and rural areas, and high schools are located at Browning, Cut Bank, Valier and Conrad.

Religious and other organizations here are similar to those found elsewhere in rural regions of the United States. Many denominations of Christian churches have followers here and each town has one or several churches. Similarly, one or several religious and secular lodges, service clubs, veterans' organizations, youth clubs, ranch, business, trade, and labor organizations are found in the communities of the area.

From this brief description it can be seen that the reservation shares a physical environment greatly similar to that of adjoining regions in Montana, and that its population participates in the life of county, state, and nation in much the same way as its surrounding neighbors. The people share in the United States economy; they work for wages, farm, ranch, and engage in the businesses, services, and government familiar to that economy. They send their children to the public schools, attend similar churches, and have in their midst the usual church, social and civic organizations. With few exceptions they wear the same kind of clothing, live in houses, drive automobiles, and enjoy the same radio and television programs. As I will show later, the expected rural American class structure appears to be present.

There are, however, some characteristics that make this area and its people different from the surrounding regions and populations. The major factors contributing to this separation appear to be:

1. A homeland has been reserved within the country for tribal members and the use and disposal of this land is restricted by governmental regulations.

2. The tribal members are defined *legally* as Indians. Like other ethnic groups, Indians are usually recognized by themselves and others as a separate social category. This is the *social* definition of an ethnic. In addition the Indian has been given a legal status which further sets him apart from the general citizenry.

3. The Indian is a conquered indigen, not an immigrant. This factor has social implications that require another study.

Reservation Population and Economy

The present Blackfeet reservation includes over 1½ million acres of land of which 936,848 acres are owned in trust status by individual Indians or by the Blackfeet tribe. Other than some reserve areas to be mentioned later, the balance of the land has been removed from trust as the Indian owners have been legally declared competent to handle their own financial affairs, and fee patent titles to their allotments have have been issued. In Indian bureau idiom, the land has become "alienated" from B.I.A. management. Some persons have retained their land in fee patent, while others have sold the land either to other tribal members, the tribe, or to whites. Approximately ⅓ of the land within the reservation is no longer owned by tribal members.[5]

The reservation also includes 4,982 acres which have been reserved by the United States for agency and reclamation purposes, and about 11,000 acres of submarginal government land leased to the tribe and re-leased by it to ranchers for grazing use. The lands have been given a use classification according to soil, vegetation, and availability of water, and the leasing of land to an ultimate user is governed by these classifications.

---

[5] These land use figures are approximate, compiled from Fagg and Associates (1970:47) and unpublished B.I.A. Budget projections. Such figures change from year to year as individuals remove their lands from trust and, perhaps, offer it for sale.

The ownership of mineral rights on reservation lands is complex. The original allotment under the Act of 1907, to be discussed later, vested both surface and mineral rights in the allottee. The 1919 allotment reserved the mineral rights of the newly allotted land in the name of the tribe. Subsequent issuance of fee patents and the sales of fee patent lands have included or excluded mineral rights according to the terms of each transaction so that no exact figure for Indian ownership of mineral rights is available.

Reservation, then, means land, "a part of the public domain, set aside for use and occupation by a group of Indians" (Federal Indian Law 1958:20). The inhabitants are not restricted to the reservation; they can come and go at will, but on the reservation they are subject to controls that have developed around use of the reservation lands. Certain legal privileges and restrictions have developed from both the interpretations of federal trust obligations and the past history of federal-Indian relations.

The Blackfeet reservation differs from the surrounding region, then, because approximately ⅔ of the land is held in trust either for individual allottees or the tribe, and its use is governed by federal laws and directives that do not apply outside the reservation. Alienated lands are not affected directly by such regulations, but a person owning such land finds that problems arising over such things as boundaries, trespass, water rights and rights-of-way involve him with trust regulations. Other ramifications of reservation land and related restrictions will be examined in what follows.

An Indian is a person defined as such by law. But the law has been built over time from decisions made in individual cases, so that it is difficult to write an all-inclusive definition. In general a person can be defined as an Indian if he qualifies on two counts: "(a) that some of his ancestors lived in America before its discovery by the Europeans, and (b) that the individual is considered an 'Indian' by the community in which he lives" (Federal Indian Law 1958:6).

A Blackfeet Indian and a member of the Blackfeet tribe is defined more specifically. Present-day tribal membership is restricted by the Blackfeet Indian Tribal Constitution to persons "of Indian blood whose names appear on the official census roll of the tribe as of January 1, 1935, . . . [and] all children born to any blood member . . . maintaining a legal residence within the territory of the reservation at the time of such birth" (Blackfeet Constitution 1936:1). No limitation was imposed by a necessary degree of Blackfeet descent or "blood" until 1962 when the tribal constitution was amended to require ¼ or more blood quantum for membership thereafter.

An Indian reservation, by its being, introduces legal qualifications that further set apart the area and the people. This is "Indian country," a concept that has been given legal currency. The definitions are diverse and complex, but in essence, Indian country is land owned by, or reserved for, Indians and subject to the jurisdiction of the United States. The reservation is one form of Indian country, and the federal government has jurisdiction over trust land and over any problems arising from its occupancy, use, or conveyance. It has reserved jurisdiction over ten "major crimes" (murder, manslaughter, rape, assault with intent to kill, arson, burglary, larceny, robbery, incest, and assault with a dangerous weapon) committed

Flood house: A typical house provided under the Rehabilitation program to replace housing destroyed in the flood of 1964.

by Indians against Indians in Indian country (Federal Indian Law 1958:320). Yet Indian country remains a part of the state in which it is located and non-Indians are subject to all state laws. Indians are subject to state laws only in matters not legally reserved to the federal government or, by its regulations, to the tribe. Indians also are subject to state law when not in Indian country. The complications arising from such overlapping jurisdictions are considered later in this chapter. (See Brophy and Aberle 1966:Chapter 2 for further discussion of these complications.)

The reservation population is quite dispersed. Many families live on their ranches, farms, or allotments along the stream valleys or scattered on the broad flats; others live in houses clustered together in towns and hamlets. Many details of both topography and settlement patterns were altered drastically in June of 1964. Heavy rains and rapidly melting snowpacks in the mountains caused major floods throughout western Montana. All creeks and rivers on the reservation overflowed their banks and two irrigation dams broke, releasing torrents of water into Two Medicine River and Birch Creek. Lives were lost and homes and ranches of many years standing were destroyed. This resulted in population shifts and changes in residential patterns the full effects of which are still evolving. One noticeable shift has been the movement of people from some of the rural districts into new homes in Browning, and similar shifts from the river and stream valleys into clusters of new houses at Starr School and Babb.

The regions of scattered dwellings are named after the rivers or creeks along which they are located—for example, Two Medicine, Badger Creek, Little

Badger, Birch Creek, Milk River—or for rail stations, schools, and historical characteristics—for example, Durham, Meriwether, Seville, Pontrasina, Badger-Fisher, and Old Agency. Browning, the agency town, and East Glacier, at the southeastern entrance to Glacier National Park, have been mentioned already. Other towns are Babb, Starr School, Blackfoot, and Heart Butte.

Babb, near the northwestern corner of the reservation, consists of scattered homes, a post office, churches, elementary school, motel, grocery store, and several cafes and bars. It serves as a tourist stop and as a community center for the approximately five hundred people who live in the surrounding countryside.

Starr School is a hamlet located seven miles northeast of Browning on Cut Bank Creek. Several houses are grouped around a school, a Catholic church, a Baptist church, and a community hall, and others are scattered up and down the creek. Since the 1964 flood the hamlet has been enlarged by the addition of flood rehabilitation homes and houses built under other tribal programs arranged in city block fashion with paved street, curbs, fire hydrants and common water and sewer service. This is a center of a largely full-blood population of about two hundred people.

Blackfoot is a rail point eight miles east of Browning consisting of a post office, stock loading pens and a few houses.

Heart Butte, in the southern tip of the reservation is another center of full-blood population. An elementary school, Catholic church, combination post office and store, a community hall, and scattered houses form the community center for the three to four hundred people living in this part of the reservation. The people go either to Browning, thirty-six miles north, or to Conrad or Valier for business and shopping requirements.

The old Cut Bank Indian Boarding School, on Cut Bank Creek seven miles north of Browning, is now a dormitory for boys and girls of elementary school age who for reasons of isolation, broken homes, or other problems cannot live at home during the time schools are in session. These children are taken by bus to the public schools in Browning.

School and community hall at Starr School.

The tribe is both a political entity with legislative, judicial, and executive powers, and a business corporation. The Corporate Charter of the Blackfeet Tribe establishes the tribe's sphere of authority over the handling of funds and the use of tribal assets for the benefit of its members. All tribal members are shareholders in the corporation and have a vote in its affairs. The nine members of the tribal council direct both the political and business affairs of the tribe and the corporation (U.S., Blackfeet Corporate Charter 1936).

Councilmen are elected by the secret ballot of eligible tribal members and serve for a period of two years. Each council supervises the voting and defines the boundaries of the election districts for the election of its successor body. Four districts are regularly recognized and each is served by an established number of councilmen. Since an amendment to the tribal constitution in 1964 reducing the Council from thirteen to nine members, Browning district is represented by three councilmen, and Seville, Heart Butte and Old Agency by two each (*Glacier Reporter*, July 2, 1964). Candidates file for election in the district in which they reside, but each voter votes for candidates from all districts. Residents of one district, therefore, may have a strong voice in deciding who will represent the voters of another district.

The tribal council elects its own officers, appoints its own court officers and police, and hires its secretarial and administrative staff. This body has been given broad powers for political and economic action within limits reserved by law to the Bureau of Indian Affairs and the Department of the Interior. Tribal actions concerning disposal of trust lands, and involving tribal credit or expenditures above an established amount are subject to review or approval by the Commissioner of Indian Affairs or his representatives.

Tribal membership legally defines a person as a Blackfeet Indian, and such membership provides a set of privileges and liabilities not shared by nonmembers. The income derived by a tribal member from crops raised on trust land, or the proceeds from the sale of stock grazed on trust land, are not subject to federal income taxes (Federal Indian Law 1958:883). All lands held in trust by the federal government are exempt from local and state property taxes. Qualified tribal members are given preference over nonmembers in the awarding of grazing or farming leases of trust land, and tribal members, like other Indians of ¼ or more degree Indian descent, are given a preference credit in applications for employment by the Bureau of Indian Affairs. These are a few of the privileges that go with tribal membership. As members of the corporation, the people also share in the earnings of the corporation. Occasionally, more frequently in the past when oil exploration was more active, the council votes a per capita payment as a distribution of tribal income in excess of that required for the operational expenses.

Such privileges are offset by some liabilities—particularly for men who feel competent to handle their own affairs. Trust lands must be leased through the agency land office and all use, leasing, procurement of fee patent titles, and sale of land come under government supervision. The man who has his land held in trust must request and receive permission to make certain uses of his land, have his plans reviewed and approved more often, go through more red tape, than the man who has a fee patent title to his land.

The allotment acts provided that the inheritance laws of the state should govern the distribution of allotted lands upon the death of an allottee. The laws of Montana recognize disposal of property by will, and the federal government recognizes the transfer of trust title, in whole or in part, by will. In the absence of a will, state laws define the succession and the share of an estate each heir shall receive. The result of fifty years or more of practice has been an increased fragmentation of original allotments to the point where an allotment may have as many as fifty owners, or have been portioned out into a series of plots too small to serve economic ends. The B.I.A. recently estimated that about 475,000 acres of reservation trust land had multiple owners (Blackfeet Agency FY 1972 Budget and Program Memorandum). The agency is charged with the duty of keeping records of such changes in ownership, and with leasing such lands for the benefit of the owners. A lease requires acquiescence of many owners and the monies received must be credited to the accounts of all heirs. Until more people make wills, and more frequently pass undivided ownership to fewer people, the land fragmentation will continue to snowball and the work load of the agency will increase in proportion. This is the "heirship land" problem that plagues the economies of most Indian reservations where tribal lands were alloted to individual owners.

The trust status of the land makes it poor security for mortgages so it is difficult for the owner of such land to borrow money for short or long-term operating expenses and capital improvements. The inability to secure ready financing, the multiple ownership situation, plus other factors that will be introduced later, have contributed to the present economic condition of the tribal members.

In 1962 I wrote:

On February 1960 in an area in which the predominant industries are agriculture and stock raising, it was reported [in unpublished tribal documents] that only 40 tribal members are farm operators, and of this number it is estimated that perhaps only 10 are farming sufficient acreage to be considered an economic unit. The farming family's income must be supplemented by wage work. One hundred and fifty families of tribal members are listed as ranchers, with an average of 85 head of beef cattle, or equivalent in sheep. A conservative estimate of the stock required for an economic unit is 100 head, so many of these people may also need supplemental income. It was estimated that another 27 families are self-supporting, or have received the financing which should make them self-supporting, in business, other non-agricultural enterprises, or as regularly employed wage earners.

In a credit appraisal of an estimated 1,200 Blackfeet families, 700 families were listed as having poor security risks. These latter had neither the experience nor the aptitude, neither the training nor the inclination, to operate a going enterprise or meet the standards of financial responsibility set by the council for prospective clients of a Revolving Loan Fund. These figures indicate that approximately 983 families of the tribe are unable to be self-supporting and depend upon casual labor, income from the leasing of lands if they have land, tribal per-capita payments and welfare for minimum subsistence.

Figures on non-Indian use of reservation land reveal the gap between Indian use and the potential of the region. Seventy-five non-Indian operators lease grazing land for stock enterprises, with an average of 5,067 acres each as compared to an average of 2,666 among the 150 Indian operators. One hundred seventy-five non-Indian farmers cultivate farms that average 560 acres each as compared to an average farm size of 200 acres for the 40 Indian farmers. The non-Indians are operating economic units on land leased from Indian owners. Many more Indian families could be self-supporting on their own land if problems of land ownership, financing, and training are ever solved, yet it is obvious that this land base is insufficient to support the population by ranching and farming alone (McFee 1962:40–41).

Comparable current figures are not available, but it is my impression that little has changed. Fagg & Associates (1970:71) report on 713 families of which 392 have incomes of less than $3,000 (median $2,716). This differs from another 1968 report showing about 62 percent of 1,830 families earning under $3,000 and a median annual income of $1,700 (Blackfeet Indian Reservation—City of Browning "Model City" Application 1968:41).

This does not mean that nothing has changed; it has. The population has increased, some people have improved their lot, and others have fallen on hard times. New ranches and farms have been started, others are in the process of breaking up. The sum of all this, however, is a rather bleak economic picture for the reservation as a whole for which there is no simple explanation. It reflects legal, social, cultural, and historical factors that I will discuss in Chapters 3 and 4.

The reservation and tribal organization bring a member into a further regional political alignment, in many respects akin to a municipal political division. The Indian Reorganization Act of 1934 and subsequent legislation have given to the tribe a broader range of powers than is usually enjoyed by a local jurisdiction. But for a few limitations and some federal review, the tribe is autonomous.

Tribal courts are given jurisdiction over civil and criminal actions brought by an Indian against another Indian. The right of jurisdiction in the case of the "ten major crimes" committed by Indians on Indians reservations has been reserved by the federal courts, but the balance of law and order matters are under tribal control. These are not subject to state or county regulation unless specifically turned over to such authorities, or shared concurrently with them, by an act of the tribal council and by an acceptance of these obligations by the county or state (Federal Indian Law 1958:319).

Non-Indians living on the reservation are subject to county and state laws and enforcement. They are affected, in addition, by tribal regulations. The tribe can regulate land use and impose taxes on nonmembers in the form of business licenses, camping fees, and hunting and fishing fees.

This overlapping jurisdiction in the area of law and order makes for a complex problem of law enforcement and requires guarded cooperation between tribal, county, state, and federal enforcement agencies. A breach of peace or a crime must be analyzed according to where it happened and who was involved in order to determine what level of enforcement has jurisdiction. Do you call the tribal police, the sheriff, the state highway patrol, or perhaps the F.B.I. agent? Actions by other than the correct officers must be sanctioned by immediate or previous agreement among the various governing bodies.

The tribal and federal regulations also affect nonmembers whenever these latter become involved in leases or other financial dealings with Indians, or where nonmembers become a party, injured or the injurer, in legal disputes, crime, or misdemeanors with members of the tribe.

Tribal members vary greatly in the degree to which they are affected by being both "Indians" and residents of the reservation. These differences are of major importance to this study and are given careful examination in later chapters. There are, however, some general results that are common to all.

There are a few times when all members recognize themselves as Indians. This unity of identification is most often expressed at tribal election time, when the rallying cry is for "Indians" to support the candidate who will protect the tribal land base from exploitation by the "white man." Indian identification comes to the fore in any discussion of land leasing and use where the tribal member may be in competition with a nonmember. Men who otherwise seldom identify as Indians remark that they have trouble in leasing land. "We Indians are supposed to have priority, but it's hard to get a lease away from a white man." Another informant complained: "I have to pay 45¢ an acre for grazing land, while the white man gets it for 31¢." I found no evidence to support this charge; the important point here is that it is "We Indians" who believe this. Members are Indians according to their interests when reservation policies and programs are considered detrimental to those interests. The government and the "white" man become the field against which common Indian identification stands out.

The tribal members are also affected when identified as Indians" by their white neighbors. A member runs the risk of meeting discrimination in social, political, and economic spheres because people categorize him, and act toward him, in terms of stereotype. He is an "Indian" regardless of the degree of discrepancy between the individual and the stereotype. Differences in physical appearance, education, speech, dress, manners, and wealth may temper the stereotyping of individuals, but the white man tends to act first according to the popular idea of what is an "Indian," and then add his qualifications: "He's a white Indian." "He's a good Indian." "Of course he is just a little bit Indian." "They are good neighbors even if they are Indians." Men of minimal Indian descent, who neither know nor express any Blackfeet cultural characteristics, are still remembered as Indians if they retain tribal membership and live on the reservation. One of these men told of a remark that came back to him after he had been given a well-earned political appointment in a town adjoining the reservation. A leading citizen was said to have remarked: "It's getting to be a fine state of affairs when we have to go down on the reservation and bring back an Indian to run that office." Differences in the discrimination encountered by tribal members will be examined in later chapters.

Summary

The Blackfeet share much of the way of life of their white rural neighbors, but differ from them by being Indians and residents of an Indian reservation. The general ecological and social characteristics shared by all tribal members have been described and some intratribal differences have been indicated. The present conditions have developed during the course of prolonged contact between the members of two societies with differing cultures—the Blackfeet Tribe and the United States.

Before examining the variation to be found among the reservation population and what this means, I will explore its historical antecedents; the Blackfeet culture of mid-nineteenth century, before the destruction of its buffalo hunting subsistence base, and the years of attempts at readaptation to the changing economy and the increased engulfment, direction and control by the white men who were the major agents for change.

3

Horse and Buffalo Days:
1850-1880

Introduction

"**P**EOPLE LIVED LONG LIVES in the old days before the white man came," said Arrowhead. "They didn't get sick in those days." Earlier I said that he and his friends were recalling a legendary past, but it was more than that. Arrowhead was voicing an old ideal. In both myth and ethnography such phrases are repeated. People prayed for protection in times of trouble, for good health and a long life. Names were given to assure these blessings. Yet people knew that in reality life was often harsh; men faced dangers in the hunt and in war; disease did strike; people became weak and infirm with advancing age. They prayed that they might escape these misfortunes. They knew too that a man would be judged to be less than a man if he failed to avenge the death of a kinsman or comrade, if he were unwilling to risk the dangers of a horse raid to acquire wealth and fame. Hunting too had its dangers, but a man must be a good provider. So children were taught to honor, emulate and support those who faced such dangers, to face up to the real world but to hope and pray for the ideal. This led to a counter view that expressed the recognition of the reality that went hand in hand with the ideal. Young men were told that it was better to die young in prestigious battle than to live on into the tribulations of old age (Grinnell 1907:189–190; Ewers 1958:103, 324). This expression of an old ideal by Arrowhead revealed a bit of the past that lives on in slightly altered form among some members of the Blackfeet tribe today. These inconsistencies were part of the reality of prereservation days, long after Indian life had been affected by European influence, yet before the Blackfeet had fully recognized the immensity of their white man problem.

The Blackfeet Indians probably saw their first white man during the mideighteenth century, and the earliest unqualified extensive record of contact was that of David Thompson, an explorer for the Hudson's Bay Company, who at the age of seventeen, spent the winter of 1787–1788 with a Piegan Blackfeet band along the Bow River in what is now southwestern Alberta (Glover 1962:48). Thompson found that horses, guns, metal, smallpox, and a few other elements of European culture had preceded him by at least fifty years as a result of contact and trade with neighboring Indian tribes (Glover 1962:240–251). The earlier indirect influence, and the later increasing association with the European immigrants led to extensive changes in Blackfeet culture, but on the whole the Indians made an orderly adaptation to the changing ecological and cultural conditions for another seventy years or so after Thompson's visit (Ewers 1955, Lewis 1942, Wilson 1963). The Blackfeet experienced a period of cultural elaboration rather than of disruption and decline, so that the Piegan and the other Blackfeet divisions—the Blood and the Northern Blackfoot, who later came under Canadian jurisdiction—were at the height of their power at mid-nineteenth century.

The closing decades of that century, however, were times of radical change. The buffalo, the keystone of the Blackfeet economy, were decimated and by 1884 the Indians had become dependent upon the United States government for subsistence. The Piegan were confined to a reservation, and both ecological conditions and the policies of the dominant society forced further changes upon them.

Seventy-five years later, when I began my fieldwork among them, the Blackfeet tribe remained in a small portion of its original territory, but the intervening events had markedly changed its composition, social organization and cultural characteristics. The tribe was no longer the homogeneous group described by the early writers. Its members reflected the years of changes brought about as people of two societies, each organized and guided by differing cultural directives, adjusted to each other and to changing conditions. Even a casual observer of the reservation scene could note a wide range of differences in appearance, speech, dress, and economic adjustment among the tribal population; could recognize some of the kinds of people described in Chapter 1.

History before 1850

The Blackfeet spoke a language of the Algonkian stock, a linguistic affiliation that has been the basis for inferring that they had migrated into the plains from the northeastern woodlands in precontact times. Early migration problems are still unsolved, but Thompson's host during his winter visit, Saukamappee, an elderly Cree living with the Piegan, recalled how in his youth he had accompanied his father and other Cree warriors on a journey to join the Piegan and other allies in an attack on an encampment of "the Snake Indians on the Plains of the Eagle Hill. . . ." The Piegan were found camped along the north bank of the North Saskatchewan River, across from the Eagle Hills (Glover 1962:241), which would place them somewhat north and west of present-day Saskatoon. Both Ewers (1955:300) and Lewis (1942:10) use this evidence to infer that this region was Piegan hunting territory early in the eighteenth century, and noting that the usual relative positions of the Blackfeet divisions put the Piegan in the van of a subsequent movement west and south to the Rocky Mountains and into what is now Montana. It was here that they were studied by Grinnell, McClintock, Curtis, Uhlenbeck, DeJong, and Wissler who visited the reservation during the two decades

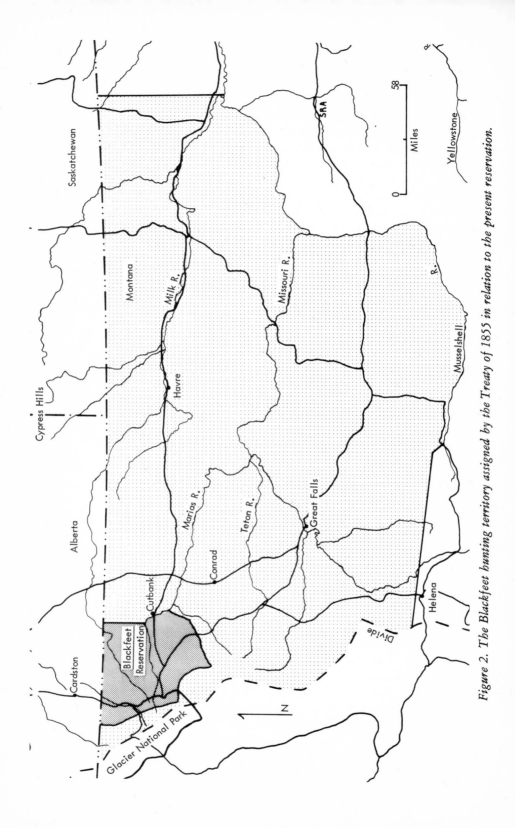

Figure 2. The Blackfeet hunting territory assigned by the Treaty of 1855 in relation to the present reservation.

following the destruction of the buffalo to study and record aspects of the classic Blackfeet culture. The following description is based upon their published works and upon the writings of Ewers who has extended and synthesized much of the earlier work (these sources are included among the Recommended Readings).[6]

By 1850, then, the Piegan ranged within a portion of the territory, roughly 27,500 square miles in extent, assigned to them a few years later by the treaty of 1855 (Fig. 2)—a hunting territory bounded on the west by the Rocky Mountains, on the north by the U.S.-Canadian border, on the south by the Musselshell River and on the east by an undetermined line at about 109.5 longitude which included the Sweetgrass Hills and the Bearpaw Mountains (Ewers 1958:122–123; Kappler 1903:553). The topography and climate was generally similar to that of the present reservation.

Economy

For the Blackfeet of prereservation days the buffalo was the major source of food, shelter, clothing, tools, and ornamentation. Ewers (1955:149–152) has given the most complete review of the many uses of the animal indicating that most all fleshy parts were eaten, sometimes raw, most frequently cooked, during the times of the year that buffalo could be hunted. Meat was dried and stored, sometimes mixed and pounded with fat and dried berries to make pemmican, both effective ways of preservation for use during the winter months when hunting was difficult. In addition, Ewers lists eighty-seven nonfood uses of the buffalo including the manufacture of tepee covers, bedding, shields, some articles of clothing, containers, straps and thongs from the hides, cups, ladles and spoons from the horns, tools of bone, fuel from dung, ornaments from hair, hide and horn and so on down to using the tail attached to a stick for a fly brush. In the trading days, too, the meat and hides of the buffalo could be used to gain guns, ammunition, utensils, knives, axes, blankets, coffee, tea, tobacco, whiskey, and clothing from the white traders. Roots, berries, elk, deer, rabbits, fish, eggs of ducks and geese and occasionally the birds themselves were used as food, and their hides, horn, antlers, bone, feathers, along with grasses, willows, and so forth, supplemented these nonfood products of the buffalo. It seems fair to say that the buffalo was the bulwark of the Blackfeet economy and, as will be shown later, much if not most of the culture—other practices, beliefs, even the values by which people were measured— were expressions of a way of life built on hunting buffalo.

The horse had assumed great importance in Blackfeet life since its intro-

---

[6] Grinnell studied the Blackfeet during the years between 1885 and 1907. McClintock first visited the reservation in 1896 and subsequently spent many summers living and studying among the Indians until 1910. Curtis was a frequent visitor between 1898 and 1910, while Uhlenbeck and DeJong conducted linguistic and folklore research in the Heart Butte and Two Medicine regions in 1911 and 1912. Wissler, with the help of D. C. Duvall, did fieldwork during the decade from 1903 to 1913. As curator of the Museum of the Plains Indian, Ewers lived in Browning from 1941 to 1944 and returned for fieldwork again during 1947. Through his own fieldwork and extensive study of ethnological and ethnohistorical sources, he has been able to extend, synthesize and reinterpret what is known of this culture.

duction to these Indians sometime between 1725 and 1750. From one perspective the horse, its ownership and use, was another hallmark of Blackfeet culture, but horses too were of value largely because of the buffalo and its place in the economy. Horses were a major tool of production.

Possession of horses increased the range and the effectiveness of hunting activities. Horses could carry more provisions than could dogs and people, allowing a man to accumulate more posessions, both material items of Indian manufacture and others gained by the more frequent and efficient trading horses made possible. At least one limitation on seasonal migrations was imposed by horse ownership. The movements of people, influenced by the migrations of the buffalo, the requirements for water, protection from the weather and enemies also had to be guided by the requirements of feed, shelter and protection for the horses.

The gun was another productive tool but did not equal the importance of horses in the subsistence pattern of the Indians, largely because the smooth-bore flintlock guns they owned, prior to the introduction of the repeating rifle in about 1870, were inferior to the bow for hunting buffalo.

In general the decisions about how many people should camp together and the techniques to be used in hunting were based on the seasons of the year and the migration patterns of the buffalo. The sequence of development of the animal from winter leanness to summer prime, the seasonal condition of hides for differing uses, the range and weather conditions and the seasonal migrations of the herds all played important parts in determining the hunting techniques to be employed.

Ewers (1955:124–129) divided the yearly round into four general divisions:

1. A winter period of five to seven months during which the small bands of Indians camped in sheltered valleys, subsisting on stored dried provisions and whatever game could be killed by small groups of men hunting on foot or on horseback, depending on the weather conditions. This was a period during which the Blackfeet were relatively sedentary, and camps were moved only as pasture, game, and fuel supplies were depleted in their valley.

2. A hunting and gathering season of approximately two months in duration started with the advent of spring. At this time of the year the buffalo began their migrations away from the sheltering river valleys toward the pastures to the east and north. The grasses and root plants began to germinate, and the Blackfeet, too, left their winter camps to hunt and collect in their separate bands.

3. During the summer the buffalo were out on the plains in great numbers, and the scattered bands of Indians came together as a tribe for a cooperative summer hunt. Buffalo bulls were at their prime during this two to three month summer season and were killed for fresh meat; hides were collected for use as robes, tepee covers, clothing and for trade. This was also the season for gathering berries and other plant products. This coming together of the bands provided for important social and ceremonial activities that I will discuss later.

4. A fall period of two to three months in length followed the breakup of the summer camp and continued until the arrival of winter storms forced the people again into winter camps. This was a season of active buffalo hunting by

individuals and small groups. The cows were in prime condition and the Black-feet concentrated on gathering the meat and berries to be dried and stored for winter use.

The most common technique for hunting buffalo during the late nineteenth century was the chase in which mounted hunters followed the herd and each man selected an animal, rode it down and killed it. By this time the Piegan had abandoned the earlier method of driving the herds into confining canyons, com-pounds or over a cliff to be killed and butchered below. Men hunted on foot only when they lacked a buffalo hunting horse, or when heavy snowfall made horse travel impossible. Although other animals might be hunted on foot, the horse was of major importance in hunting buffalo—the Blackfeet "staff of life."

Horses, then, were a form of production capital, and their importance led to another form of economic pursuit, the horse raid. A man could build a horse herd by buying animals from his neighbors, by having them given to him, by natural increase among his already acquired stock, or by raiding and taking horses from enemy camps. This was a dangerous but quick way to build capital, and success in such dangerous pursuits added to a person's prestige, so horse raiding became ". . . an established industry among the Blackfeet" (Grinnell 1907:244).

Labor was quite sharply divided by sex. Men were the hunters and de-fenders, women the collectors and manual laborers. In addition to hunting and fighting, men butchered the animals while on the hunt, made their weapons, shields, and drums, and painted designs on these. They also made pipes, horn utensils and often their own ornaments, leggings, and coats.

Women's work makes a longer list. They occasionally helped with light butchering when they accompanied a hunt, but did all butchering, preparing and preserving of meat once it had been brought to camp. Women gathered plant foods, prepared meals, made the clothing, packed, moved, and unpacked provi-sions and possessions, carried wood and water, cut tepee poles, put up and dis-mantled the tepees, made and decorated leather carrying bags (parfleches) and other containers, manufactured utensils, dressed and tanned skins and hides, made saddles and horse gear, made travois, and reared the children.

It would appear that the women did the most "work," which may be over-looking the fact that hunting, an avocation for us, was often an arduous occupation. Nonetheless, it was true that men had more time for socializing. Young men often dressed up in their paint and finest clothing, to stroll around the camp in order to be admired by the girls; and the older men spent much of their leisure time in feasting one another.

A similar division of labor and male advantage was a part of childhood. Young boys were free to play, until as they grew older they were given the task of caring for the horses. The games they played were preparation for hunting and raiding. At a much earlier age girls began to carry wood and water, do light gathering and collecting, and take lessons in the preparation of foods, clothing and in dressing hides—learning the women's work.

The Blackfeet were much concerned with personal property and had their own definition of what it entailed. Resources were unowned, food and materials were open equally to all according to one's energy and ability. Tribes, bands, and even families might have their favorite and usual area within which to hunt, but these ties to a territory were unrelated to ideas of ownership of land, game or plants. Once labor had been expended, however—an animal killed, a horse stolen, a plant gathered, a stick or stone picked up, or a dream dreamed—the product was imbued with value and became personal property.

It is possible to separate food from other types of property because it was not owned by individuals in the same way as were other goods. Food "belonged" to the collector but was put in charge of the women of the collector's own or adopted family upon return to camp. Food then belonged to the family, yet even this title was clouded by a series of social obligations. A hunter was obliged to share with anyone who had helped him in the kill, with the man whose horse he had borrowed, or with the man from whom he had obtained hunting power. He was expected to provide some part of the meat for the sick or disabled, and he also might have had obligations to some of his in-laws. The family used what remained. In times of famine these rules were set aside and food became band property to be shared by all. Food had additional uses, both ceremonial and social—feasts were an important part of many rituals, to be described later, and as part of the everyday social life of the men, as noted above.

Horses and other goods were individually owned by men, women or children. Personal dreams, experiences, exploits, and the symbols of these were also personal property and all could be transferred—sold, exchanged, given, or loaned, in whole or in part—by one person to another. These other goods appear to have been free of forced sharing in times of scarcity. The rule appears to have been that none should starve, but other needs of the poor had to be met by appeals to the generosity of those who had more. The unfortunate were cared for but usually given worn or castoff clothing, tepee covers, tools, robes, and so on, rarely things of much value.

Goods other than food were used by their owners or were used as exchange goods. Exchange might be for economic reasons, as when a man gave a horse to a medicine man for a cure, or to get a charm to insure success in horse stealing, war, or other endeavor. Goods might be given in exchange for the supernatural power of another. One kind of property could be used to purchase another, for example, furs and guns for horses, or horses for tepee covers. Another type of transfer was for ritual reasons, as when goods were offered to the sun in the Sun Dance, to ghosts or other spirit forces in propitiation, petition, or thanksgiving. Here too could be classified the practice of placing some of the property of a deceased with his body in order that he might have the use of such things in the next world.

A third use, more difficult to classify, would be the exchange of property in gambling. The Blackfeet were avid gamblers and some on occasion were known to have gambled away all their possessions.

The fourth use of property was its transfer, by gift or exchange, in order to gain increased prestige and status. Among the Blackfeet property was accumulated and wealth created, to be used for the demonstration of generosity. A man secured horses and other goods in order to give them away. He loaned a horse to another hunter, in part to share in the meat, in part to create an obligation for a repayment, but this act was also a display of generosity toward one of less wealth and thus established a moral obligation that could be converted later into support for one's opinions in council. A man of property gained position within his band by sharing generously with those less fortunate than himself, and gained stature within the tribe by feasting members of other bands and the giving of gifts to the leaders of other bands. *Generosity was a major requisite for prestige and status.*

In summary, resources were unowned, food and materials were open equally to all according to his energy and ability. Food became the property of the one who took it, to be shared first with his family, then with others to whom he might be obligated and with the unfortunate. In times of famine, food became band property to be shared by all.

Horses and other material goods were individually owned and were bought and sold, borrowed and given. Personal dreams, experiences, exploits and the symbols of these were also personal property and could be transferred by one person to another in exchange for other goods.

The distribution system fostered individual gain and accumulation. The consumption system countered this by imposing social sanctions that rewarded charity and generosity with prestige and status. This force will be examined further.

Social Organization

A child born to Blackfeet parents began early to learn the patterns of social interaction. He was first of all a member of a household—the occupants of a single tepee—which included the parents, unmarried brothers and sisters, and perhaps one or two other relatives as well, such as a grandparent, a maiden aunt, or other wives of the household head.

As the child grew older it learned that its family was the minimal economic unit of the Blackfeet society. The father was the decision maker, the one responsible for the protection and good behavior of its members; the first wife was the owner of the tepee, responsible for the other wives if any, for the care of the children, maintenance of the tepee and other duties within the women's realm. The child learned too about other kinsmen, that he had important relatives on both sides of the family—in other words, kin were recognized bilaterally.

As acquaintances were made beyond the household, he or she learned that there were other families that regularly lived near and traveled with one's own. These were members of the band, the day in and day out hunting and gathering group that was the basic economic and political unit of the Blackfeet. It was the band that moved according to the requirements of the yearly round, camped alone through the winter, joined with other bands in the summer for the tribal hunt. The child learned the band name and identified with it: he was a child of his parents and one of the Small Robes, Skunks, Lone Eaters or whatever his band might be (see Grinnell 1907:208–210 for one listing of band names). Over the years he learned too that the people who gathered during the summer hunt were fellow Piegan, and that among other people encountered on occasion were some who spoke his language, did things his way, were Blackfeet of the other divisions—the

Siksika and the Kainah—who often came to the aid of the Piegan in times of conflict.

While kin ties were basic to band formation, friendship and self-interest played a part as well, and people changed bands when they felt it advantageous to do so. Ewers believes that this shifting band allegiance had developed with the inequal distribution of wealth that followed the acquisition of the horse. Poor people became more dependent upon the generosity of the wealthy few and attached themselves to the bands of those men who could best provide for them.

Band membership then was based first of all upon kin ties, but with no absolute rule of descent. Wives usually joined the band of their husbands and children belonged to that of their father, but it was not unusual for a man to join his wife's group. A widow could choose to remain in her husband's band or to return to that of her parents. A man could change band affiliation "even in middle life . . ." (Wissler 1911:19). Other persons attached themselves to the band for various reasons, and long residence with a band, and acceptance by its members, was tantamount to band membership.

The tribe was a larger association of individual bands whose members recognized common ties of language, kinship and culture. It was an organized unit only during the few weeks of the summer hunt, and tribal discipline operated only at this time. Even here the bands retained their spatial and functional autonomy; each band had it habitual place in the camp circle and continued to operate as an economic and political unit with only a part of its powers surrendered to the tribal organization.

Like other Plains Indians, the Piegan had a series of men's organizations, or societies, of which there were three basic types: age-graded warrior societies, religious societies and cults, and the less formal dance association.

The named warrior societies (Mosquitoes, Pigeons, Braves, All-Crazy Dogs, etc.) were corporate groups, that is, they continued over time, surviving the individual members. Groups of young men of a similar age sometimes started a new society, or, more usually, got together and bought memberships in an ongoing society. Similarly the old members would in turn buy into the next age-rank. The transfer was between individuals and such purchases could occur at any time. It was customary, however, for several men to transfer at the same time. Periodic transfers of this kind made possible a progressive movement of membership from a lower to a higher ranking society as men grew older. The oldest society might continue as its ranks were renewed from below, or eventually die out as its members passed away.

These were the groups granted policing powers at the summer encampment. In addition they served to promote the military spirit of the members through war games and intersociety competition in races, dancing and games.

The medicine men's societies and related cults were less formally organized gatherings of men who owned important medicine bundles and powers. These men conferred together to aid in the organization and presentation of the Sun Dance and to promote the spiritual and material welfare of the tribe. The dance organizations were social clubs made up of young men who organized for the purpose of staging social dances during the time of the summer encampment.

Membership in one or more of these organizations created loyalties that cut across the ties of kinship and band affiliation, and helped to contribute to tribal solidarity. In other words, a person identified first with his kinsmen and with his band, but later established additional and potentially conflicting ties of loyalty by marrying someone from another band and by membership in a society that drew its members from many bands.

Band and tribal leadership was not inherited but open to all who could command a following. A band headman gained a position of influence by displaying the qualities (see below) valued in his society and by his continued exercise of these attributes. His influence depended upon his power to persuade others, and the support of many followers increased this ability. He conferred with family heads and all decisions were reached by mutual agreement.

Band leaders formed a council during the tribal encampment and one of them, by election or selection, came to be considered the chief of the tribe. The chief had no institutionalized authority and little disciplining power. His chiefly functions were to guide the council to agreement and to mediate in cases of conflict and uncertainty.

There were no formalized institutions for social control except for the policing duties of the associations under special regulations put into effect at the summer encampment. Conflict was first of all a matter between individuals, then a concern of the families and finally of the bands. The delinquent person was cautioned, ridiculed, gossiped about, and shamed into conformity. Ostracism and violence were the ultimate penalties within the band, but usually gossip and shame served to restore order. Boys and girls growing up in Piegan society were urged to achieve the ideals of that society. Boys were told to be brave, to be good fighters, able to defend themselves against their peers and to protect younger children. They were praised for skills and daring, even for sexual exploits. Girls were urged to be quiet, dutiful, sober, hard-working, and to protect their virginity.[7] Both were rewarded with praise when they achieved, and punished with sarcasm and gossiped about when they misbehaved or failed. These sanctions contributed to a developing concern with their own identity and to a strong sense of shame, and such concerns in turn gave added force to these mechanisms of social control. Gossip and shame were also used to curb intratribal conflicts among adults. A cluster of tepees made an ideal setting for effective ridicule. Wissler (1911:24) describes a process of "formal ridicule" that was used to curb "mild persistent misconduct." When the people were quietly settled in of an evening, a headman would call out to a neighbor asking him if he had heard about that silly fellow two tepees down who had been mistreating his wife? Men in other tepees would join in telling what they thought of the man and his behavior, all to the discomfort of the victim and the enjoyment of everyone else. Sarcasm, ridicule, and the accompanying laughter, added up to an evening of entertainment for all but the victim, who was soon highly motivated to mend his ways.

---

[7] The double standard in ideal sexual relations set up some strains; in order for one sex to achieve the other had to fall short of the ideal. I gather from the literature that there was a mix of failure and success in the attainment of these ideals on the part of both boys and girls (Ewers 1958:98).

In the more serious cases of adult disputes, force and physical punishment were employed if gossip failed. In cases of murder, a revenge killing might take place if a high payment was not offered in retribution and accepted. A person who disrupted the summer hunt might be beaten and have his clothing and weapons destroyed. An adulterous woman might have her nose cut off, or be put to death by the members of her husband's warrior society (Grinnell 1907:220, Ewers 1958:97–98; Wissler 1911:24–26 discuss specific punishments).

These forces contributed to the development of some general personality characteristics of the Blackfeet. Grinnell found them, like other Plains Indians, to be "talkative, merry, and lighthearted," and fond of joking, even though they appeared reserved and quiet when with strangers (Grinnell 1907:181). Wissler commented on their fondness for jest and practical jokes (Wissler 1911:52–53). In addition, I get a picture of a brave, resourceful people, industrious and aggressive, yet much concerned with self, jealous, and easily shamed. These characteristics and their expression were further reinforced by the Blackfeet beliefs.

Religion

While learning all these skills and rules, the young people were learning as well the beliefs that gave the practices validity, supported the rights and privileges of age, gave meaning to the Blackfeet world, and added supernatural reinforcement to the moral code.

All of the Blackfeet universe was invested with a pervasive supernatural power that could be met with in the natural environment. A man could seek and avail himself of this power through proper behavior and ritual. He went alone to a remote place to fast and pray, and to await the dream or vision that would transfer power to him. If he was successful the supernatural appeared to him, usually in animate form, and promised aid and success in all or specific endeavors, if the man in return would observe faithfully a series of taboos and periodically re-enact in ritual the experience by which he had received the power. The spirit-being instructed the petitioner to make a medicine bundle containing the symbols of his power and taught him the appropriate songs and rituals. The spirit was now his guardian and could be called upon for protection in times of trouble.

The powers, paraphernalia, and rituals became the personal property of the owner. He and the spirit dealt with each other as individuals, and any group benefits to be expected from this relationship were dependent on the inclinations of the individual owner. The complete power, bundle, songs, and ritual could be sold, or transferred, by one individual to another for a price. The owners of some bundles could sell short-term benefits of their power, as well, usually by going through the ceremony of the bundle for the benefit of an individual, the family, band, or tribe, or through the preparation of a charm to be used by the purchaser. Ewers relates how Wolf Calf acquired horse medicine power and how he used it, how he transferred parts of the power and how these parts and the bundle itself were transferred to a series of men from those days in the early nineteenth century on up into the time of Ewer's informants of the 1940s (Ewers 1955:258–261). The point here is that these powers and their symbols were subject to the same controls as any other property. A man, therefore, incurred both rights and obligations with the attainment of power. He was expected to be generous with it, but at the same time he expected to be paid in goods or prestige for the help he gave.

The Blackfeet believed that the possession of a guardian spirit and power were important for success, so such powers and the bundles that represented them were highly valued. Not all men were successful in their vision quest, but this was not held against them. They were just unlucky. Neither they nor anyone else expected much of them, however, and they could hardly advance in prestige without some successes. Such men might be motivated to gain property to enable them to purchase power from someone who had had the experience, and men with power often sought to transfer it because it was a restricted and often burdensome property. As with other kinds of property, the bundle owner was expected to be generous with his power. Bundles had to be opened periodically, and the owner had to provide a feast for invited guests as a part of the ritual. In addition, the bundle owner had to observe a number of taboos associated with each bundle—it had to be displayed properly, no one should walk between the bundle and its owner, and numerous restrictions were put on the owner's behavior. Some men owned several bundles, but whether one or many, some owners found the responsibilities, expenses and taboos too burdensome and sought buyers for their power.

Values and Status

Perhaps, as already indicated, one of the most persistent themes of Blackfeet life was the high value put on individual prestige, a value that operated through and maintained a status structure. This was not a true class society with easily recognized social divisions, but a structure of status positions, each shading into a higher one. The high status people were distinguished readily from those of low status, but the separations along the line might be imperceptible.[8] The whole system was an expression of Blackfeet values, and the highest status was achieved by the man who best represented these ideals.

The major characteristics valued by the Blackfeet and by which men were judged appear to have been bravery, generosity, wisdom, and skill; these were displayed in warfare, horse raiding, hunting, religious knowledge and the acquisition of property for use in the service of others.

It is difficult to establish a hierarchy of the importance of these different attributes. Bravery and generosity appear to have been essential. The ethnographers differ in their ordering of exploits by which a reputation for bravery was established, but all agree that war honors were ranked, and that the killing and scalping of an enemy ranked below the more dangerous feats of successfully wresting the weapons from an enemy and escaping without injury, or stealing into the center

---

[8] Ewers believes that social classes were forming in the late 1880s under the influence of horse ownership. A small rich class, a numerous middle class, and a number of poor were recognized, grounded in respect for individual rights and property rights (Ewers 1955:240–244).

of an enemy encampment and making off with a fine horse that had been tethered to its owner's tepee. Bravery was measured, then, according to the relative danger of the exploit and the most dangerous deeds were those related to war and raiding. But brave deeds alone were not enough. Unless a man were generous with his goods and helpful to his neighbors, he would be branded as selfish and stingy and his supporters might abandon him. This emphasis put stress on acquiring property with which to be generous which in turn made skill important. But all these traits were enhanced if a man had supernatural support. Power increased a man's self-confidence and the expectancy of success on the part of himself and others. Ewers remarked that the horse raider ". . . was a courageous, alert, resourceful fighting man. Nevertheless, he did not attribute his success in war to these qualities. Rather he attributed it to the power of his war medicine" (Ewers 1958:127).

A man of ability, achievement, and with supernatural support was able to attract followers in his ventures of war and raiding, or in his political maneuvers. Influence began to build as he used these qualities and property to rally members of his family and band. He drew first upon the ties of kinship and then attracted followers from other groups to gain leadership within the band. The maintenance of this position, and the advance to higher status depended upon his ability to exercise all of his personal attributes in correct ways.

The ideals were a standard, of course, and probably few attained the ideal. But those who did stood as examples to the children, as noted earlier. People measured each other and themselves by the ideals, and in a society where gossip was an important control over behavior, verbal praise was eagerly sought. What people said about you was important, and the amount of praise a person received could be increased if he spoke well of himself. This seemed to be a response among the Blackfeet. People talked about their good deeds as well as the good and bad deeds of others, and were much concerned about their own good name. Men who aspired to leadership tested each other's claims; while rising on their own claims they could climb faster, in a relative sense, if by gossip they could cut down the man above them.

In a sense then, property was the measure of a man's achievement, and the use of property became the means of validating a particular status and rising to a higher one. Property was accumulated to use in the gaining of further goods and, above all, as a means of expressing generosity. Highest status went to the generous man; a stingy man was the butt of gossip, and lost status among the Blackfeet.

Claims of power, bravery, skill and generosity were subject to public judgment. Opportunities were given, particularly at the Sun Dance, for the recital of coup claims, and public acceptance of these served to validate them. Men called upon to fill the roles in the Sun Dance ritual, society initiations, and naming ceremonies were selected from among those of accomplishment, and before performing the required act the man recounted the achievements that qualified him for the honor being bestowed upon him. Similarly, the woman who sponsored the Sun Dance, and the women who cut the buffalo tongues as a part of the ritual, publicly proclaimed their virtue. In ordinary conversation and in the give and take of daily life people might boast and overelaborate their exploits, but in these formal situations they tended to curb such over-enthusiastic self-appraisal. On these occasions anyone who knew such claims to be false or exaggerated was expected to challenge the claim. A woman who came to cut the tongues, for instance, would not only have claimed to have been a good hard working wife, free from the charge of adultery, but would also have related, naming names, the occasions on which she had resisted seduction. "You, Brave Eagle," she might have said, "You remember how you surprised me last fall when I was picking berries, and tried to get me to commit adultery. I told you off, didn't I." If she had told the truth, Brave Eagle would have had to confirm her statement; if she had lied, he would have had to contradict her. After all, his manliness was being attacked—if she was right he lost status as a great lover even as she gained or retained her prestige as a virtuous woman. Concern with self, public proclamation, and public validation kept people from making false claims. They advanced by validating deeds and virtues and by exposing the false claims of another.

Summary

The Blackfeet culture was based upon and integrated with a hunting and gathering economy in which the buffalo was most important. The hunting band was the major economic and political unit. While the band was essentially a kinship group, people did change bands when it was to their advantage to do so. A band leader held his position by popular support, and gained power in tribal councils according to the number of followers he had. Power and leadership were exercised through persuasion and influence. No one could dictate and important decisions were reached by unanimity.

Both private ownership of property, other than land and resources, and the rights of the individual were held in high esteem. People strove to accumulate property, but material wealth was not the goal. Rather, property was given away to exhibit generosity.

Generosity, bravery, wisdom, and skill were highly valued personal qualities. War, horse raiding, hunting, and religious practice provided the major avenues for the achievement and display of these values. Men used bravery and skill to acquire fame and property, and they sought, or bought, supernatural power to aid in these endeavors. They used their gains to exhibit wisdom and generosity in order to attract a personal following that would lead to increased influence and higher social position.

The loss of the buffalo seriously undermined the whole culture. The Blackfeet faced radically altered conditions of life and were called upon to make unprecedented changes. New subsistence techniques were necessary. New skills had to be learned and old ones became obsolete. Economic dependency led to the loss of much political, religious and social autonomy. The following chapter is used to trace the readaptations that accompanied the events subsequent to this catastrophe.

4

Dependency and Readaptation: 1884-1970

Introduction

THE UNSUCCESSFUL HUNTS of 1883–1884 marked the end of the subsistence pattern on which the Blackfeet had built their culture. The Indians scoured the region for food, and moved in around the agency to ask for help from the agent. In Blackfeet culture those who had food shared it during times of want; the agent supposedly had food and as a leader he was now expected to validate his status by caring for those who had none. The United States government had acknowledged responsibility for the Blackfeet in the 1855 and subsequent treaties, but agency supplies were inadequate to meet famine conditions. Up to ¼ of the Piegan perished during the winter of 1883–1884 (Ewers 1958:293–294).

The Indians had to find a new and meaningful subsistence base as well as new ways in which to express old values and to maintain prestige and status. At the same time, the government, upon which they were dependent, pressed them to accept new value and prestige systems, quite different from their traditional ones.

The following historical review of the Blackfeet adaptation and adjustment since 1884 includes a statement of the general objectives and attendant values expressed in United States Indian policies of the period, a presentation of the means used to further these aims, and the Blackfeet reactions to them during (a) the period of dependency to 1935, and (b) the period of self-rule under the Indian Reorganization Act from 1935 to the 1960s.

United States Indian Policies

The prevalent policy of the period emphasized the eventual "civilization" and assimilation of the Indians, although the means to these ends were often diverse and inconsistent. There appeared to be general agreement by this time that the Indian could be civilized most effectively through education and agriculture. The Indian Commissioner, in his report for 1885, made an impassioned plea:

> It requires no seer to foretell or foresee the civilization of the Indian race as a result naturally deducible from a knowledge and practice upon their part of the art of agriculture; . . . those races who are in ignorance of agriculture are also ignorant of almost everything else.

> It should be industriously and gravely impressed upon them that they must abandon their tribal relations and take lands in severalty, as the cornerstone of their complete success in agriculture, which means self-support, personal independence, and material thrift.

The Indian, he continued, must be taught to work, to send his children to school, and to seek "material independence" (U.S. Comm. Ind. Affairs 1885:III–V).

Two major themes alternated in ascendancy throughout eighty to ninety years of attempts to achieve this goal for the American Indian:

1. The end could best be accomplished by drastic pragmatic programs intended to produce a quick cure regardless of the expense in individual maladaptation.

2. Progress could only be made slowly through humanitarian programs that would allow for gradual, individual readaptation and assimilation.

The goals, and the two approaches to their implementation are expressed well in the following statements selected from Senate debates over the question of allotting land to individual Indians.

The goal was restated eloquently by Senator George H. Pendleton of Ohio in 1881:

> . . . we must encourage them to industry and self-dependence . . . and we must stimulate within them . . . the idea of home, of family, and of property. These are the very anchorages of civilization; . . . (U.S. Congressional Record XI 1881: 906).

The short term approach was advocated by Senator Henry M. Teller of Colorado in 1886:

> I suggested on a former bill the opening of the country, putting side by side with the Indian farmer of a white farmer; . . . Give to our people, . . . the right to go upon the Indian lands and make, side by side of the Indian farm, a farm tilled by the aggressive and enterprising Anglo-Saxon, and in a little while contact alone will compel these people to accept the civilization that surrounds them on every side (U.S. Congressional Record XVII 1886:1762–1763).

Senator John T. Morgan of Alabama advanced the humanitarian viewpoint:

> The measure which the Senator proposes here must be one of growth. Of course we know that all this western country at some future day must be populated jointly by Indians and white people; but until the Indians get into condition where they can be protected against the white men who would sell them whiskey,

. . . powder and shot, and out-deal them in all their transactions, it is the duty of the Government of the United States to preserve them in some form or other until they have matured sufficiently to become able to control their own domestic affairs, and manage their own property (U.S. Congressional Record XVII 1886: 1764).

These two themes will be seen to alternate in ascendancy in governmental policies from that time to the present. The goal of eventual assimilation has been questioned seriously only in the last forty years. The debate culminated in the passage of the General Allotment Act of 1887 that authorized the President to permit the allotment in severalty of reservation lands to Indians (U.S. Statutes XXIV 1887:388).

The values stressed in that policy are work (industry), self-dependence (self-support), individualism (independence of the tribe), and acquisitiveness (implied in home-building, material thrift, and private ownership). These are some of the qualities valued by the culture-bearing agents of American society who came into long and continuous contact with the members of the Blackfeet tribe. The Americans apparently gave little thought to either the preservation of the Indian value and status systems or to ways in which these might be used to implement governmental policies. The Blackfeet probably thought of the whites as a minority group who had promised to help them and turned to the white man for help with little thought that Indian values were in serious jeopardy.

The following review of the history of United States-Blackfeet relations from 1884 to 1970 attempts to trace the interplay between the American and Blackfeet value systems during the course of economic readaptation. The events of history tend to be those seen and recorded by whites, and for many years even the thoughts of the Blackfeet had to find expression through the white man's pen.

The Period of Dependency, 1884-1935

1884-1891 Following the winter of 1883-1884 the first efforts of the agents were directed toward relieving the famine and providing for the future sustenance of the people. A new agent made his first report in the fall of 1884 in which he wrote that he found few results of past efforts to make the Blackfeet sedentary and self-supporting farmers (U.S. Comm. Ind. Affairs 1884:106-108). During the next six years the agents attempted to build up the agency farm and herd, to encourage the Indians to raise grain and produce, and to forward other programs of "civilization."

From this time on, the dependent Blackfeet were subjected increasingly to the American concepts of law and order. The Indian police, under the agent's direction, were instrumental in eliminating warfare and horse raiding. In 1888 the agent reported that Indian "depredations" had ceased and there had been no horse "stealing" during the preceding year (U.S. Comm. Ind. Affairs 1888:152). American pressure against war and horse raiding had eliminated two more traditional avenues to the acquisition of property and prestige; hunting, as a major expression of skill, had already lost its place in Blackfeet life.

In his report of 1888, Agent Baldwin was less optimistic about the agricultural possibilities on the reservation than he had been in previous years (U.S. Comm. Ind. Affairs 1888:150–152). The crops failed in 1889 and 1890, and in 1891 the agent reported that no crops had been planted in the past year either by Indians or by the agency because of fear of further drought (U.S. Comm. Ind. Affairs 1891:265).

In 1888 the agreement whereby the Blackfeet relinquished claim to the lands to the east of the present reservation boundary was ratified by Congress. In return the United States promised annuities, in the amount of $150,000 for a period of ten years, to be paid in the form of goods and services necessary for Indian progress toward civilization (U.S. Comm. Ind. Affairs 1888:303).

The first ration of cattle and horses under the agreement was issued in 1890. Agent John Catlin summed up the preceding five years of agricultural endeavor as "commendable," but wrote that the Indians had experienced failure "through no fault of their own." The Indian interest in stock raising led to his recommendation that grazing be given precedence over agriculture in future programs (U.S. Comm. Ind. Affairs 1890:114). Efforts to establish farming as an economic base had met with little success.

1892–1905   By 1892 the Piegan herd had been built up to 6,827 head of cattle and 4,616 head of horses. The Indians were moving out over more of the reservation and claiming land in anticipation of eventual allotment. They were beginning to establish herds, build houses and corrals, and to shift the emphasis of cultivation to raising hay for the stock (U.S. Comm. Ind. Affairs 1892:280–281, 807). Each subsequent report emphasized the suitability of the area for stock raising and reported a substantial increase in the Indian herds.

In 1898 a severe winter and a shortage of feed caused a 40 percent loss among the Indian cattle, and the irrigation engineer for the agency recommended extension of the irrigation canals in order to increase hay production (U.S. Comm. Ind. Affairs 1898:187–188). Indian ranchers, however, had a chance to recover from this setback. Additional cattle were included in the annual issues and stock raising continued.

An agreement for the sale of the Rocky Mountain portion of the reservation was approved by the United States government in 1896 (U.S. Statutes XXIX 1897:353). The conditions of the sale assured another ten years of annuities after the obligations under the 1887 treaty had been met.

By 1904 the agent reported a total of 20,509 head of cattle and 12,000 head of horses owned by the Blackfeet, and claimed that only 10 percent of Indian subsistence had been dependent upon government issues for that fiscal year (U.S. Comm. Ind. Affairs 1904:610–611, 600). Thus in the first two decades of dependency Blackfeet had tried farming and experienced failure. They were then encouraged to try stock raising and had begun to make some economic adaptation as herdsmen.

Their *cultural* readaptation, up to this time, had been less successful than the economic development. The increasing settlement of the lands around the reservation and the efforts of the police, as noted earlier, had ended horse raiding. Christian missions, particularly from the Roman Catholic church, had been intermittently active among the Piegan for several decades, but Father Imoda had discounted their success at conversion prior to 1870 (Bradley 1923:316). In 1890 the Holy Family Mission school was opened in the Two Medicine valley (U.S. Comm. Ind. Affairs 1890:115) and in the following years Christianity gradually gained predominance over the Blackfeet religion. In the meantime, agents, missionaries, and teachers actively combatted any expression of many elements of Indian culture.

> Sun dances, Indian mourning, Indian medicine, beating of the tom-tom, gambling, wearing of Indian costumes . . . selling, trading, exchanging or giving away anything issued to them have been prohibited, while other less pernicious practices, such as horse-racing, face-painting, etc., are discouraged (U.S. Comm. Ind. Affairs 1894:159).

In addition, the children were forbidden to speak the Blackfeet language in the schools (U.S. Comm. Ind. Affairs 1893:174). Several informants, who attended either agency or mission schools during the first decades of the twentieth century, recall being punished for "speaking Indian" in the schools or dormitories.

The suppression of elements of culture that the white men thought were inconsistent with civilization did not eliminate the practices, but did hamper and limit their expression and transmission. The readaptation process was slow, but the agents usually found some grounds for optimism.

1905–1920   Progress in stock raising continued through 1905 and 1906. The agent persistently attempted to keep encroaching herds off Indian pastures, and continued a practice begun in 1904 of issuing leases and permits to both white and Indian stockmen for grazing privileges on tribal lands.[9]

The economic growth was again reversed by a severe winter in 1906 and 1907. The losses among the stock were heavy and "impoverished some of the industrious and worthy members of the tribe" (U.S. Comm. Ind. Affairs 1907:13–14). An investigation into conditions on the reservation was ordered, and the investigating officer's report sheds some light on the progress of economic adaptation to that time:

> He reported that the mixed bloods—about three eighths of the tribe—were able generally to take care of themselves, but the full bloods as a rule had little knowledge of ranch or farm work, were unwilling to stay a reasonable length of time in one place or to work where they could not be in parties, were very apt to quit on little or no provocation and regardless of the interests of the employer, . . . (U.S. Comm. Ind. Affairs 1907:13–14).

A federal act of March 1907 provided for the allotment in severalty of the Blackfeet reservation. Each tribal member would receive 280 acres of grazing land and 40 acres of irrigable land, or 320 acres of grazing land only. Surplus lands would be opened for public settlement. An appropriation was included for the construction of an irrigation system for the lands to be allotted; the money

---

[9] The first such permit recorded was for a five-year lease of 2,400 acres to the Conrad Investment Company (U.S. Comm. Ind. Affairs 1904:77). An increasing number of leases are reported for most of the following years.

appropriated to be reimbursed from proceeds of the sale of the surplus reservation lands (U.S. Statutes XXXIV 1907:1015, 1035). Allotment surveys and work on the irrigation projects were carried on during the two years following the enactment of the legislation (U.S. Comm. Ind. Affairs 1908:61; 1909:4–5). Irrigation construction provided an additional source of labor and income for many Indians.

The last annuities under the agreement of 1896 were paid in 1908. Henceforth Indian rations and aid were dependent upon tribal income, reimbursable government appropriations, and occasional relief measures. The statistics from the agents' reports for the next few years give a picture of continuing economic progress for the tribe as a whole.

The First World War relieved some of the pressure on reservation resources —good weather and abundant crops prevailed generally until 1917; livestock and produce found a ready market at high prices; and many Blackfeet were drawn into the armed forces, thereby reducing the local labor force. But all of this does not reflect accurately the condition of individuals. A process was going on that was slowly segmenting the population.

First, the population was growing—from 2,063 in 1905 (U.S. Board Ind. Comm. 1905:facing 16) to 2,957 in 1920—and becoming increasingly hybridized. White men were marrying the Indians' daughters. The full-blood Blackfeet loved the grandchildren these marriages produced, but they were "half-breeds," and hard to accept as "real Indians." Of the total, in 1920, less than half, or 1,141 persons, were full-bloods, while the balance were mixed. Among the mixed-blood population, 956 were ½ or less Indian (U.S. Comm. Ind. Affairs 1920:67). Secondly, the individually owned herds were growing and the returns from this business were high, but as the superintendent wrote in 1918, 3 percent of the tribe owned 95 percent of the stock when he reported for duty in 1915 (U.S. Congress Sen. Report 451 1918:3). An investigator for the Board of Indian Commissioners, in November of 1918, found that the full-bloods were divided as to their capabilities as stockmen. He reported that "about one-third of the 300 and more full-blood families is incapable of handling cattle." Another third probably could become cattlemen if properly instructed and supervised, and the balance of the full-bloods were doing well at the industry. A number of mixed-bloods had built prosperous looking ranches and had had "marked success at this business" (U.S. Board Ind. Comm. 1918:352–353).

Other forces were already at work that were to alter the uneven progress of the Blackfeet. Beginning in 1917, the Indian Bureau began pressing for the rapid reduction of Indian dependency by the removal of "competent" Indians from trust status (U.S. Comm. Ind. Affairs 1917:3–5). By 1920, 1,011 Blackfeet had been awarded fee patent title to 312,250 acres (U.S. Comm. Ind. Affairs 1920:171) under a policy that was to result in the alienation of reservation lands and the creation of a large number of landless Indians.

A drought cycle began in 1917 and continued for four years (U.S. Board Ind. Comm. 1921:55; Whetstone 1956:145–146). The end of the war, in 1917, resulted in the loss of markets. The drought and falling prices brought bankruptcy to both cattlemen and farmers in this part of Montana by 1919 and 1920. Veterans returned to swell the labor force. The Blackfeet shared in this change. The white homesteaders and cattlemen could abandon their places and go elsewhere; the Indian could not and had to rely again upon the government (U.S. Board Ind. Comm. 1921:56). The Indian, however, did have the agency to turn to, an advantage not shared by the white man. During the winter of 1920–1921 rations were issued to "over 2,000, or about two-thirds of the entire population" (U.S. Comm. Ind. Affairs 1922:12). Several informants reported that their families and friends were ruined at this time. A few were able to make a comeback, but many abandoned their ranches and did not try again.

In 1919, a second allotment of reservation lands was authorized in the annual appropriation bill for the Bureau of Indian Affairs (U.S. Statutes XLI 1919:16–17). After this no further allotments in severalty were made to the Blackfeet Indians.

The Blackfeet generally were dependent again. Thirty-five years of attempted economic readaptation were behind them. They had tried farming and found it unrewarding. They had found satisfaction in stock raising, but only a few were able to succeed at this in the face of cold winters, periods of drought, and the fluctuating markets regulated by national and international conditions. Large numbers of younger men had been employed in seasonal labor, railway and irrigation construction work, harvesting and ranch labor and had served in the armed forces. These jobs provided some cash income but little training for long-range adjustment. Unused allotments were leased to others to provide another small cash return to the Indian owner. Many people depended entirely upon the rations issued and the cash that could be earned by wage work or leasing of land.

Periodic crop failures and price fluctuations made it difficult for the Indian to understand or to develop faith in long-range plans. Each government program offered future rewards and security, but the promised rewards never materialized; the only tangible things were cash, rations, and relief. The white man's values of thrift and hard work had been developed and maintained by a better than average experience of success; few Blackfeet, by 1920, had experienced enough consistent reward to become imbued with these values. Every ten years or so their best efforts had resulted in failure.

1920–1935   The next fifteen years were in many ways a repetition of the the past, and reinforced more than they changed the expectation patterns. Montana farmers, generally, experienced a severe depression during this time (Montana Almanac 1957:122) and this was capped by the national depression and the droughts of the Dust Bowl years that began in 1929 and 1930 (Toole 1959:240).

In 1921 a new and dedicated agent, Frank C. Campbell, began a "Five Year Program" of subsistence farming and economic development financed by reimbursable Indian bureau funds. He visited each Indian home and by consultation won support for his program. The Blackfeet were given a sense of participating in the planning of their own economy. The agent consulted with them and made a place for indigenous leaders with whom the people could discuss and resolve their problems (U.S. Board Ind. Comm. 1923:47; 1925:22–23).

Campbell remained with them until 1929. His program benefited many people, but others wanted more independence. They wanted to restock and operate their ranches, to continue their own operations with a minimum of governmental interference (Ewers 1958:322–323). Nevertheless, the Five Year Programs gave many persons a sense of accomplishment and helped carry the Indians through a period of widespread hard times.

The wholesale granting of competency and fee patents was halted in 1926 when it was recognized that "the lands of a vast majority of Indians who had been given absolute control of their allotments [had] passed from Indian ownership in various ways . . ." (U.S. Comm. Ind. Affairs 1926:10–11).

The cycle of success and failure was not broken by the Five Year Plans, however. The enthusiasm of both the Indians and the agents died down during the years between 1929 and 1935 and the greater number of the Blackfeet returned to economic dependency (Ewers 1958:323).

In 1933 the Works Progress Administration (W.P.A.) and the Civilian Conservation Corps (C.C.C.) programs were established to meet national unemployment and the benefits were extended to Indian reservations (U.S. Sec't. Interior 1937:218). Like the irrigation construction of earlier years, these programs provided a source of seasonal cash labor, an important prop to the economy, but one that provided little training for permanent employment on the reservation.

At this point in Blackfeet adaptation, new national Indian policies were being formulated. The Meriam Report, a monumental study of the Indian problems published in 1928, questioned the whole doctrine of assimilation of the Indians.

> He who wishes to merge into the social and economic life of the prevailing civilization of this country should be given all practicable aid and advice in making the necessary adjustments. He who wants to remain an Indian and live according to his old culture should be aided in doing so (Meriam 1928:28).

This, and many other of the recommendations, became official policy with the passage of the Indian Reorganization Act in 1934 (U.S. Statutes XLVIII 1934:984). The act provided, among other things, for the cessation of allotment of Indian land, a limitation on the sale of restricted Indian land to other than tribal members, and the establishment of a revolving loan fund from which Indian corporations could borrow to further either tribal or individual enterprises. Tribes were authorized to organize and to adopt a constitution, and those who organized were given broad powers of self-government previously denied to them. Organized tribes were also empowered to incorporate and manage tribal properties and income. Actions of both the political and business organizations were subject to approval and review by the Bureau of Indian Affairs.

In addition, the traditional cultures were given recognition for the first time. A circular sent to all agencies in 1934 illustrates the sharp reversal from previous communications about Indian cultural practices:

No interference with Indian religious life or expression will hereafter be tolerated . . . and it is desirable that Indians be bilingual. . . . The Indian arts are to be prized, nourished, and honored (U.S. Sec't. Interior 1934:90).

The Indians were to have a choice, and to be allowed to play some part in decisions about their future development.

The Period of Self-Government, 1935–1970

The Blackfeet Constitution and the Blackfeet Corporate Charter were accepted and approved in 1935. The population continued to grow: the report for 1935 lists the membership of the Blackfeet Tribe as 3,962, of which 561 were living outside the reservation jurisdiction (U.S. Sec't. Interior 1935:163). The economy improved slowly after the bad years of the early thirties. The stockmen, in particular, were aided by a provision for a repayment cattle pool authorized in 1934 (see U.S. Sec't. Interior 1937:212–213 for repayment in kind program, and 1944:241 for a review of the program). A man could build a herd by borrowing cattle from the pool and repaying in kind from the increase.

The Johnson-O'Malley Act (U.S. Statutes XLVIII 1934:956) passed in 1934 and amended in 1936 (U.S. Statutes XLIX 1936:1498) authorized the Secretary of the Interior to contract with a state or other political units, and with schools, colleges, and private corporations for educational and medical services, agricultural assistance, social welfare, and relief for Indians. The Annual Report for 1934 stated that the Browning schools were assuming the task of educating the Blackfeet children from that district (U.S. Sec't. Interior 1934:85).

The majority of the Blackfeet still were attempting to readapt to the immediate present, to find success in a new economic endeavor. They were pressed to close a wide cultural gap in a short period of time, and to make things more difficult, the national economy would not stand still. Ranching and farming were changing in both production and marketing practices. A writer for the *Montana Almanac* noted a trend away from subsistence farming in the 1920s as homestead holdings proved to be too small for efficient farm and ranch operations, especially with the increasing use of power machinery in subsequent years (1957:202).

The Indian's future on small subsistence farms of 80 acres, or on a ranch using a 360 to 420 acre grazing allotment, was not promising. A successful operation required the use of leased land and adequate capital. The heirship status of individual trust lands made leasing difficult, and trust restrictions inhibited the mortgaging of such lands. The day of slowly building a ranch or farm from a cow, some seed, and hard work was disappearing. Few Blackfeet were established sufficiently in the 1930s to build and maintain a remunerative enterprise.

From 1936 through 1940 general drought conditions continued in the region (U.S., Indians at Work IV, 7 1936:37, 8 1936:37–39; Toole 1959:240— for Montana from 1929 to 1939). A few men held onto their farms and ranches, but most were forced to rely on wages from occasional labor and welfare payments. One report stated that general poverty was the lot of ¾ of the Blackfeet people in 1936 (U.S., Indians at Work IV, 4, 1936:38).

An additional source of unearned income was provided when the Indians were declared eligible for Social Security benefits by an act of 1936 (U.S. Statutes XLIX 1936:620). This provided categorical aid to the needy, blind, aged, and the dependent children. In 1939, 91 old persons, 186 children, and 3 blind persons on the Blackfeet reservation received this help (U.S. Statistical Report 1939:15).

From about 1936 on, the impact of modern medicine began to be felt by the Blackfeet. The agency physician reported an increased desire for obstetric service, "an increase from an average of ten a year to 127 in the fiscal year for 1936" (U.S., Indians at Work IV, 4, 1936:39). A new hospital was opened in 1937,[10] and during the fiscal year 1940 a staff of twelve served 1,181 patients in addition to providing dispensary treatment to 5,204 cases. Five field employees administered to an additional 4,945 (U.S. Ind. Affairs Stat. Supplement 1940:82). C.C.C. nurses and Red Cross workers were also tending to the health of the Blackfeet (U.S. Sec't. Interior 1937:218). The medicine men were losing their hold. By 1959 informants reported that all the Indians used the Public Health Service hospital and medicines. Only a few medicine men were left and while they did some curing, they too went to the white doctor on occasion.

The tribal council attempted to further self-help improvement projects using revolving loan funds appropriated by Congress. The Office of Indian Affairs encouraged other enterprises by providing farm and home extension workers to advise the farmers and ranchers, and to organize women's community clubs for instruction in homemaking. The extension agents encouraged the growth of 4-H clubs to teach agriculture, stock raising and homemaking to the boys and girls (see reports in U.S., Indians at Work III, 12, 1936:43; and in U.S. Comm. Ind. Affairs 1936:179–184; 1937:211–217).

By 1941, the eve of World War II, the Blackfeet had made but slow recovery. The long-range economic problems had not been solved. They, like other Indians, were still leasing the land to others rather than using it themselves (U.S. Sec't. Interior 1941:451–452). The C.C.C. remained an important economic prop.

The war years, 1942–1945, had far-reaching effects on the Blackfeet. The C.C.C. program was suspended in 1942 (U.S. Sec't. Interior 1943:317), but several hundred young men and women served in the armed forces and worked in defense plants around the country (Ewers 1958:324). The "greatest exodus of Indians from reservations that has ever taken place" occurred during the war years (U.S. Sec't. Interior 1944:237). Indians were meeting other Americans, learning new skills, and seeing more of the outside world. Ready markets and higher prices for farm products coincided with increased rainfall to bring general prosperity to the Montana farmers and ranchers (Toole 1959:241), and the Blackfeet shared in this.

Like all past periods of activity and increased economic advance, this one met reversals after the war. The greater number of the Indians returned to the

---

[10] Reported under construction (U.S. Sec't. Interior 1936:175); all hospitals under construction in 1936 were reported completed in 1937 (U.S. Sec't. Interior 1937:234).

reservation when the military forces were demobilized and the war industries were closed (U.S. Sec't. Interior 1946:353). Wage work fell off and a "downward trend in family incomes set in" (U.S. Sec't. Interior 1946:351).

The young people returned with money to spend, but the opportunities for investment were scarce. Few of them owned land with which to start a ranch or farm. They had the money to build new homes, but again no land of their own upon which to build. Not many had the experience and motivation to overcome these handicaps.

While the Indians were readjusting to peace time reservation life, the general U.S. population was expanding, both in numbers and in movement of population. The demands for new land revived pressures for the removal of trust restrictions on Indian land (U.S. Sec't. Interior 1951:368–369). Once again there was an increase of fee patent awards and the sale and alienation of more land.

The council and the agency persevered in endeavors to resolve the reservation economic problems. Stock raising and agricultural programs were initiated, and national programs for relocation and on-the-job training for Indians were pushed. By 1949 the cattle holdings of the Blackfeet had increased to 14,678 (U.S. Sec't. Interior 1950:356), but the figures, as usual, do not tell the whole story. As in the past, only a few were able to keep a ranch going over time to remain as one of the 150 families engaged in stock raising in 1959. Accounts of informants' experiences during this period show some of the personal and tribal problems of adaptation during the postwar years.

> I started years ago to build a herd with repayment cattle. At that time they accepted repayment as a man was able to make it. I took ten years to pay back fifty head. Then they made changes and required that repayment be made within two years. One bad year made this impossible. 1947 was a bad year. The people needed hay to get their cattle through the winter. The government wouldn't finance feeding. Then, because the Indian wasn't able to feed, they came in and hauled away the cattle. I managed to borrow $700 from a friend in town and made it through the winter.
> —a presently successful rancher, mixed-blood, leasing 2,400 acres.

> My father had a ranch and I helped him from the time I left school until the war. After the war I got a job in California and stayed there until my father asked me to come back and help with the ranch. I worked on the ranch for two years, then my father, who was getting old, sold off his stock in 1948 and I went to work for another rancher.
> —a steadily employed farmhand, ¼ Blackfeet.

> I had a good herd and then got sick and couldn't take care of them. Nobody would. Some were stolen so I sold them all.
> —a full-blood pensioner.

> My father bought this land and is leasing more to farm. I dropped out of school to help and now I'm running the farm. My father got a F.H.A. loan to improve the house and we're doing good.
> —a young farmer, ⁵⁄₁₆ Blackfeet.

> I was farming, had 80 acres of grain but that wasn't enough to make a living. Then I ranched on the 580 acres. I had sixty-five head, including calves—loan cattle. The loan requirements insist that you stay with the cattle, but I took wage

jobs to make enough to live on, so they took my cattle. Just didn't have enough land for farming or ranching.
——a seasonally employed construction worker, $\frac{1}{16}$ Blackfeet.

I have about thirty-five head I'm running with family stock on other people's land. These are loan cattle. I've been taking five to ten head a year and haven't been pressed for payment. Just pay them back when I can. The family helps take care of them. I want to lease some land but I find it hard to do. The Indian gets priority but somehow it seems hard to get land away from the white lease-holders.
——a regularly employed carpenter, $\frac{1}{4}$ Blackfeet.

I was raised on a ranch. Before the war I was living and working for my uncle who had cattle. I had some loan cattle and was just getting started. Then I was called into the Army. They only kept me six months, but no one would take care of my cattle while I was gone so I turned back the loan cattle and sold the rest. After the war I came to town and worked for wages.
——an irregularly employed laborer, full-blood.

This is the way these men see the problems, and whether or not they are correct in their appraisal is beside the point. The important thing is that, for various reasons, many men failed to make a go of ranching and farming while a few others did. The successful ones appear to have had family support. Only by cooperation, in which some of the family took wage earning jobs while others tended the ranch, were most enterprises kept going.

The pressure for ending trust status of Indian land culminated in the adoption of House Concurrent Resolution 108 in 1953 calling for the "earliest possible" termination of federal responsibilities over specified Indian tribes (U.S. Congr. Record XCIX, 8, 1953:9968). The Blackfeet were not included among the Indians to be "freed," but the resolution was interpreted as a statement of intent to end rapidly the trust status of all Indians. In response to this resolution, the

issuance of patents in fee nearly doubled as compared with the previous year . . . while the disposition of allotted holdings through advertised sale more than tripled . . . (U.S. Sec't. Interior 1953:24).

A brief moratorium in effect during 1958 was lifted the following year "in complance with a congressional request. . . ." (U.S. Sec't. Interior 1959:253). The Blackfeet continued to lose reservation land to nonmembers.

While federal and tribal authorities were attempting to increase the industrial capacity of the reservation, other forces were working against them. The population was growing—from the 3,921 resident members in 1941 to 4,850 in 1960 to more than 6,000 by 1970. The increasing number of Blackfeet who had left the reservation often included the most educated.[11] The land sales and continued fractionization of allotments through inheritance procedures made land consolidation and utilization increasingly difficult. The trend toward larger farms

---

[11] This out-migration continues, largely because there are few opportunities on the reservation for turning learning into income. Weber tried to find a correlation between schooling and income among his Babb sample and concluded that for making money ". . . in a community with very few jobs other than those demanding physical labor, comparative youth and vigor are more important than variations in schooling" (1969:16).

and ranches increased the need for additional capital, but funds were not available to meet the demand. Periods of declining employment, that is the recession of 1957–1959, cut into individual earnings from wage labor. No new proven oil fields had been tapped, and interest in oil exploration decreased. When individual and tribal earnings fell off, the demand for welfare funds increased. The council contributed the greatest share to the county welfare program, so the relief the people received was yet another drain upon tribal income.

Tribal self-government suffered under these pressures. It was difficult to get a majority of the tribe to support any political or economic measure. The council, itself split on issues, despaired of tribal unity:

> Members of the Blackfeet Tribe are generally very poor. Their income is meager and consists mostly of income from leased trust land, casual labor, and participation in Tribal programs operated with Tribal income.
>
> It is very difficult to convince these people that Tribal income should be assigned for any purpose. Most of our people see only the spectre of having their income, and consequently Tribal programs and their direct benefits, diverted into programs designed for only more progressive members of the Tribe. To these people, it is a matter of personal survival. Any possible reduction in Tribal income to them automatically means a reduction in personal income.
>
> . . . until at least thirty per cent of the adult population of the Tribe becomes self-supporting and thus able to plan and to think in terms of the future, it appears that programs requiring popular approval for use of locally supervised Tribal funds will certainly be limited to those programs which meet the daily emergency needs of members of the Blackfeet Tribe. (Letter from the Secretary of the Blackfeet Tribal Business Council to the Commissioner of Indian Affairs, March 3, 1960, Blackfeet Tribal Council Documents.)

Consequently, long-range programs were often deferred, per capita payments were made, and in most cases, the recipients spent the money for immediate needs.

The pessimism reflected above should be tempered, however. Even as he wrote the letter, the tribal secretary and other councilmen were working on plans for improving the housing on the reservation. Following councils, in face of continuing criticism by many tribal members, invested money in programs to develop tribal resources and provide more opportunities for employment on the reservation: one of the first fruits of this effort was the establishment of the Blackfeet Forest Products Enterprises in 1963. This group was funded by the tribe in the amount of $10,000 and given the authority to lease a mill site and to award a franchise for the erection and operation of a sawmill to a private operator. The mill was to hire local help and to use logs cut by Blackfeet labor from the tribal timber holdings. Mill operations have suffered from breakdowns because of the age of the equipment acquired; several operators have taken the concession and given it up in the face of difficulties; but the mill continues to operate, troubles are being ironed out, and the hours of work available to local men has gradually increased to the point that the sawmill and attendant timber cutting operations appear to be a small but important prop to the local economy.

With a tribal investment of both land and money, and a loan from the U.S. Economic Development Administration, the Business Council has developed an industrial park adjacent to the railroad just south of Browning. The council, with the help of the Browning Industrial Development Corporation formed by private citizens both members and nonmembers of the tribe, has actively sought to attract small industries to the industrial park with some success. One industry, a wood products prefabrication plant, is presently in operation, constructing houses for tribal housing programs, and negotiations continue with other potential occupants.

The tragic flood of 1964 had left 129 families homeless. An emergency appropriation to the B.I.A. provided 5.5 million dollars for relief and reconstruction of homes, roads, dams, and canals on the reservation (*Glacier Reporter,* August 20, 1964). By late October 1964 the first units were being fabricated and hauled to the home sites in the old communities (*Glacier Reporter,* October 24, 1964). Some families chose not to move back to the old location and had their homes erected in city block patterns in Browning, Babb, and Starr School. In many, but not all, instances the new homes were roomier and provided more modern cooking and sanitary facilities than had been the case with the houses they replaced.

Good homes have been scarce on the reservation for many years, with only 32 percent of Indian families living in sound housing in 1969 according to a B.I.A. estimate (**FY 1972 Budget and Program Memorandum**). Housing programs developed by the Blackfeet Indian Housing Authority have been making

Several generations of housing: One log house has been renovated and expanded under a B.I.A. Home Improvement program.

New home constructed by the owner under the Mutual Aid Housing program.

an impact, however. Low-rent home consruction programs have been funded by the U.S. Department of Housing and Urban Development; fifty such units were completed and accepted in 1966 and another fifty-five were nearing completion during the summer of 1970. Construction had started during that summer of fifty middle income rental homes financed by a tribal investment of land and F.H.A. supported loans. In another program, the Housing Authority, supported by the U.S. Federal Housing Assistance Administration began Mutual Help Housing construction. The first units under this program were occupied in 1965 and additional units have been completed and occupied in each succeeding year in Browning, Babb, and Starr School. This is a cooperative endeavor drawing on the resources of many agencies. The F.H.A.A. made a loan for the purchase of material and wages for supervisory labor, the B.I.A. provided general supervisory help, the tribe through the Housing Authority selected the candidates for home ownership. The purchasers contributed their labor to build their own house and to help their neighbors, and agreed to pay off the loan with small monthly payments geared to the family income. No one buyer could occupy his house until all houses of any one segment of the program were finished. These projects take time; the faster builder awaits the slower, but with cooperation the job gets done.

Other tribal investments of land combined with federal loan programs have resulted in the completion of a new tribal office and community center and a new modern jail.

The attention of both the tribe and the B.I.A. has recently turned to the development of the tourist potential of the reservation. For many years the Blackfeet have been aware of the tourists. Many have earned money as entertainers at the lodges of Glacier National Park, others have profited from the sale of Indian crafts to tourists passing through the reservation to and from the park. The Museum of the Plains Indian has attracted an ever increasing number of visitors since its opening in 1941, and the Blackfeet Arts and Crafts Association has supplied and sold local Indian work through the museum gift shop and through its own shop at St. Mary. Duck Lake in the northern part of the reservation has long been famous as a fishing spot and attracted its share of travelers. But it is becoming apparent that the tourist potential has hardly been tapped. Plans are well along for a major tourist complex, with a lodge, campground, dining facilities, bar, marina, Indian tepee village and other facilities on Lower St. Mary Lake. Some camping facilities are already available and others are being planned. Such enterprises will surely produce revenues for the tribe; how many jobs will result for tribal members is another question. Concessionaires often bring their own employees in spite of efforts by the tribe to guarantee these jobs to local people.

Head Start, Community Action Planning and other ventures supported by grants from the U.S. Office of Economic Opportunity continue to relieve some of the problems of the tribe; yet much needs to be done. I feel a sense of optimism about the future, but find this feeling difficult to support except for certain material signs of an improved economy—new buildings, homes, roads and services. For many people, however, the basic problem of a meaningful job and a reliable income seem as far away as ever. New industries help, but still do not provide jobs for all who need them among a growing population. Employment reports still show high unemployment and a primary dependence on firefighting and other seasonal and sporadic kinds of wage labor for jobs. Robbins's study of the Heart Butte region does little to allay these fears. He reported that only 50 percent of the cash income reported by the members of his sample came from employment, another 20 percent derived from land leased to others and 30 percent of the income for these households came from welfare funds (Robbins 1968:198). Heart Butte is not representative of the whole reservation, but may well indicate the economic conditions in the underdeveloped rural areas.

A similarly gloomy view is expressed by local people in an application for the support of a Model Cities Program:

> The lack of Employment Opportunities is basic. Year round jobs are scarce. Available opportunities in this area are mostly seasonal, thus throwing many workers into a low income bracket. This is true of Indian and non-Indian alike. Jobs that do become available are oftentimes accompanied with unrealistic requirements, i.e., setting educational levels too high, years of experience for the job too extreme, or emphasis on racial preferences.
> There are not enough diverse fields of interest—no technical challenges. Work categories are numbered and few. Economic resources are undeveloped to a great extent. . . . Training is limited particularly in specialized fields. . . . Poor work habits must be overcome as job and training opportunities come forth. . . . A careless attitude has built up along with the feeling of uselessness. . . .
> The role of the male is decaying in the home due to this feeling of uselessness. The woman has taken on an increasing role in family providing and management. The male role must be revitalized if there is to be job success. Learning skills would be an encouragement. . . .
> Low income is prevalent on the Reservation, particularly among Indian families. Approximately 62% of the resident Indian families have annual incomes below $3,000.00, and the mean income is $1,700.00. It has been estimated that approximately 3,000 persons receive some form of welfare financial assistance during part of each year. In the case of large families, the assistance standards are sometimes actually competitive with available earned income, since many local jobs, cowpunching for example, pay far below minimum standard wages. . . .

The overall picture is one of widespread economic impoverishment which in the case of many families is shared with emotional impoverishment. As is true among most people who live in chronic poverty, the poor people of the Reservation have a feeling of hopelessness and helplessness in controlling their own destiny (Blackfeet Indian Reservation—City of Browning "Model City" Application 1968: 39–41).

This must be read as a portion of a document requesting economic assistance; nevertheless, the problems are there and the solutions will not appear immediately. The much-maligned councils are working on long-range programs that appear to offer promise of improvement, but they do this in the face of continuous opposition from those tribal members, both on and off the reservation, who want tribal spending cut and income distributed in per capita payments instead of being invested in industrial developments. The tribal council is severely criticized by its constituents and accused of everything from mismanagement to out-and-out graft. Some of these charges might be true, but I think it is important to note that this is a tribal body, elected by the tribal members, attempting to deal with local problems under the surveillance of local people. In this respect it is much like local governing bodies anywhere else in the United States. I think it is better for the Blackfeet to be at work solving their own problems through their elected representatives than to have these tasks turned over to either private or federal "experts" and all of the accompanying elaborate bureaucracy.

Overshadowing these economic and political problems and pervading all decision and debate is the concern about "termination." Termination is sometimes defined as the withdrawal of federal responsibilities for Indians, at other times as terminating the special relationship between the federal government and Indians. Its proponents usually talk about giving the Indians the full rights, privileges, and responsibilities of their citizenship. Usually these words are pronounced with less stress on "responsibilities" than on "rights" and "privileges," because the main responsibility to be gained is that of paying land and income taxes, a responsibility that has been denied the man who kept his land in trust. To most Indians termination signals the abrogation of long-standing treaties and the removal of federal protection from unfriendly and rapacious whites who "really only want to take our land away from us." Land is, perhaps, the one remaining tangible tie to the past, as well as an emotionally loaded symbol of Indian identity. Indians criticize the B.I.A. but resist its abolishment. It is the only remaining defense between them and termination, and when someone says "termination" the Indians hear "extermination."

Summary

The emphasis, in this chapter, has been upon the economic problems of Blackfeet readaptation following the depletion of the buffalo. The pressures put upon the people, both directly and indirectly to change other parts of their culture can be summarized now and related to the problem of the maintenance or replacement of the traditional value and prestige systems.

The end of the hunting economy made hunting skills obsolete. Migratory seasonal dwelling patterns lost their function. Dependency undermined band and tribal leadership. Warfare and horse raiding were stopped. A man no longer was able to exhibit bravery in the hunt, in war, or on the raid. He no longer could use these means to acquire property with which to display generosity.

Other cultural characteristics were seen to have been under strong pressure. Indian beliefs, religion, ritual, curing practices, and some aspects of social life had been discouraged or outlawed for many years. The acceptance of hospitalization and modern medicine reduced the importance of Indian curing as a channel to prestige. The conversion of many people to Christianity, and the suppression of religious expression and ritual undermined these beliefs and practices. The religious avenues to status were slowly blocked.

Many people remained committed to the old values but were hard pressed to make economic adaptation and at the same time express the traditional values. Generosity could still be practiced, but even this was made difficult under the new conditions. The practice of generosity often blocked the economic success the Indians were asked to achieve. A good and generous man could not hoard his cattle when his family and friends were in need, yet if he was generous with his stock the herd was depleted and his enterprise failed. The qualities that bolstered prestige among the Indian-oriented militated against gaining prestige among the white-oriented, and vice versa.

There is, to be sure, another side to the coin that must be recognized. Reciprocity was important to the survival of the poor. This tended to support and even generate generous behavior, making it difficult for me to decide whether the present stress on generosity is a carry-over from the old days or a response to modern conditions. Probably both factors are present in the patterns of daily reciprocity; cultural persistence seems evident in the rhetoric of generosity and surely most apparent in the give-away ceremonies.

The increased hybridization of the population was noted. This contributed to quite divergent home environments and socialization practices among the tribe.

All of these factors resulted in differing economic, social, and cultural accommodations among the tribal members. A few succeeded and many failed in subsistence endeavors. In varying degrees, some people retained Indian beliefs, practices, and values, while others turned to new ways. Still other members of the tribe, mainly mixed-bloods, learned little or nothing of Blackfeet culture but were socialized in white ways.

Some of the results of these processes were described in Chapter 2. In the following chapters I examine the present community in more detail, to show the type of social organization that has evolved in order to accommodate the varied sociocultural combinations that have developed during eighty-six years of change.

5

Intratribal Diversity

Introduction

TWO SOCIETIES EACH ORGANIZED AND GUIDED by different and often conflicting cultural directives came into contact, and it was this that set in motion the processes of change reviewed in the previous chapter. The Blackfeet were dependent and subordinate. The institutions involved with Indian affairs were charged to assimilate the Indians, and in this they have been partially successful. The Blackfeet tribe of today is recognizably different from the tribe of the past. Houses have replaced tepees, automobiles and farm machinery have made the horse relatively obsolete. Subsistence is gained within a money economy at ranching, farming, business, services or wage labor. Schools, churchs, and other institutions of the general white society are supported. Most people speak English, all dress like their non-Indian neighbors. Perhaps most surprising is that anything of the traditional Blackfeet culture remains in light of the concerted effort that was made to stamp out these traditions, yet much persists.

It is my thesis that the present Blackfeet tribe represents a bicultural and bisocial community. Albert Buffalo Heart and Henry Rogers represent life styles too divergent to be fitted into one social network, or even into one cultural tradition. Two societies and two cultures remain, localized on the reservation, all embedded in the wider state and national milieu. The larger theme of two societies in contact, interacting and changing, is reproduced on a smaller scale within the tribal membership.

This division appears to be recognized by the people themselves. In the local idiom, people are either "full-bloods" or "mixed-bloods"; or at other times are classed as "real Indians" or "assimilated Indians," but these labels do not cut the tribal membership domain in the same ways. By descent an "assimilated Indian" frequently turns out to be a full-blood, or the "real Indian" is found to be a mixed-blood. Essentially both sets of stereotypes recognize two differing life styles, which at first seem easy to explain as two different responses to change. One group, it might be said, is made up of the "progressive" members of the tribe who have accepted more change than the "conservative" or "traditional" segment, which has resisted change. Anthropologists have sometimes used these labels to describe social divisions within Indian reservation communities. This process of differential acceptance and rejection of change has played a part in the evolution of the Blackfeet community, but other factors have also been at work to further complicate the matter.

One complicating factor is the presence of numerous tribal members of ¼ or less Indian "blood," who cannot be considered as Indians, or as members of families that have become assimilated. In one sense they are Indian only by the grace of one Indian grandparent or great-grandparent. Yet they live on the reservation and play an important part in tribal affairs. At one point I thought I could distinguish three categories: "real Indians," "assimilated Indians," and "Indians by technicality," but the last named do not form a distinct social group. They interact with the "assimilated" people and share a common culture. I gradually came to recognize that there were really two relatively distinct social divisions within the reservation community and named these the *Indian-oriented* and *white-oriented* societies. These cumbersome but appropriate labels recognize the cultural "directions" toward which the people in each group are oriented.

Many interrelated processes have led to this condition. In the preceding chapter culture change was described in terms of the development of the tribe as a whole in response to historical events. Another view of the same events could be taken from the perspective of the individuals who made their own adaptation and accommodation to the changing conditions of daily life. From this position the differential experience of persons with the two cultural systems, in home, school, church, work experience, and travel, seems most important. Of these the socialization experience in the childhood homes looms large when seen in the continuity from child to parent to grandparent back through time to the buffalo days. A few sketches from representative family histories should serve to indicate the complexity of the transmission processes that maintain and perpetuate the two social divisions in the reservation community.

Socialization to White-Orientation

A middle-aged full-blood man, who I shall call Ray Hawkins, told me about his childhood home and training. His parents saw the end of the buffalo days and concluded that the old life was ended. He remembers his father telling him, "The Indian days are gone. In a few years he will be only a thing in a museum that people will pay to see. You must live like our white brothers." His parents took up ranching and brought in a white tutor to teach the children English and other things they needed to prepare them for the new life ahead. Ray recalled that the tutor brought "books, a blackboard, chalk, paper, and pencils and set up a real school with recess and all." The children seldom left the ranch and were not allowed to play with other Indian children. "We were scared of the Indians," this full-blood told me, "If they came near the house we would hide under the bed." Later they were sent to school in Canada. Both his parents and the school stressed the values of hard work, honesty, thrift, and education, and this man and his wife have been guided by these principles in the raising of their own children.

This case represents an abrupt break in the continuity of socialization and is an example of one way by which a full-blood family can move from Indian to white orientation. Missionary and governmental attempts to gain the same result by removing Indian children from their parental homes and into boarding schools failed more often than not. Perhaps the change occurred in this case because the parents had made the choice; they changed their own living style, and withdrew from contact with many of their past kin and social ties. They further insured the change by providing the tutor and the schooling that gave the children the experiences the parents were unable to supply, that prepared them for a way of life so different from what the parents had known.

Other paths to white-orientation are discernible in the life stories of some mixed-bloods. Oscar Swanson is $\frac{1}{16}$ Blackfeet and his paternal grandfather was an immigrant from Sweden who came into Montana in the late 1890s as an employee of the railroad. He married a mixed-blood woman and they built a successful cattle ranch. Oscar's father was raised on the ranch and evidently learned very little of the Blackfeet culture from his mother. This seems to have been a common pattern in such marriages, even where the mother was a full-blood. The man was boss, he set the goals for the family and the Indian wife supported these. In some cases the wives were the driving force that made their white husbands successful. Oscar's mother was the daughter of a white family that had come from the midwest to homestead just east of the reservation. She and Oscar's father had gone to school together and were married soon after their eighth grade graduation. These two continued the ranch operation and raised their children in the way of life they both knew. Consequently, Indian traditions, language, and beliefs are strange to Oscar. He is one of the "Indians by technicality" who qualifies for tribal membership because his great-grandmother was a Blackfeet, and he resides on the reservation. Like Robert Thompson, described earlier, he feels that being part Indian has had little effect on him; life would have been much the same if he had been born and raised just off the reservation by white parents. His children, now $\frac{1}{32}$ Blackfeet, continue in the patterns of socialization established by their parents and grandparents, yet remain as members of the tribe because they were born prior to the restrictive amendment to the tribal constitution.

Many of the white-oriented members of the tribe are from similar background, but the variations are interesting and show the international influences that have affected reservation life. Anthony Garceau, an elderly cattleman, was the son of mixed-blood parents. His paternal grandfather was a French fur trapper who married a Canadian Cree girl. Their only son, Anthony's father, was raised in a trading post. He went to school for a few years, worked for the trader for a time and then started ranching in southern Saskatchewan. Anthony's mother was born at Fort Benton, the daughter of a Piegan girl who had married another French immigrant fur trader. Her mother died when she was a child, so her father sent her to a convent in Winnipeg where she was raised and educated. At about the age of eighteen she visited friends in Saskatchewan where she met and married

Mr. Garceau. Shortly after Anthony was born, his father died and his mother brought the children to the reservation where she worked in the schools to support them. Neither parent had learned to speak their native Indian languages, so French was the language used in the home. The Garceau children, along with their Blackfeet-speaking friends, learned English in school.

Anthony left school while still in his teens and began ranching on his own. He experienced all the ups and downs of that industry, but rebuilt after each loss and gradually established a successful cattle ranch which he managed until old age and infirmities made it necessary for him to turn the operation over to his sons. His children were raised in a home and educated in schools that provided no influences from traditional Blackfeet culture.

Several other genealogies show a similar history indicating that people from many parts of Europe and the United States have contributed to the genetic and cultural mix that makes up the present Blackfeet tribe.

Another successful white-oriented rancher, Harry Wilson, recalled that

> My grandfather, old man Wilson, originally came from England. He was in the army sent out to Alberta to pacify the Indians. He married a daughter of one of the chiefs he had fought against. Later he moved the family to Fort Benton where he set up a trading post. My father was raised there and came to the reservation just after the turn of the century, where he married my mother, a white woman.

This man, again, was one of a second generation of mixed-marriages where the white parent stayed to direct the training of the children to ranch life. But Harry had an experience not shared by others of his family. His paternal grandfather died, after which his grandmother married a Blood Indian and went to live with him in Alberta. Harry went to visit them when he was still a young boy and stayed for three years, where he became a favorite of his stepgrandfather who set out to make him a medicine man. He learned much of the lore, customs and ritual from the old man and was allowed to participate in many of the ceremonies. He remembers that by the time he came home he could speak Blackfeet fluently and had almost forgotten how to speak English. He inherited many of the old man's things and remembers much of what he learned during that visit. Harry learned to appreciate the Indian traditions and he retains an empathy with and understanding of the Indian-oriented that allows him to participate legitimately in some of the rituals.

After his return home, he entered again into white-oriented life, became a successful rancher both on and off the reservation, has held political offices and been a 4-H leader. He married a white woman and they have had five children all of whom have been raised in white ways. This family too is listed on the tribal roll and those who have remained on the reservation play a part in reservation life.

Harry's experience in two traditions has not been unique among the white-oriented of his generation. Two cases come to mind where the mothers of children in their teens were remarried to full-blood men following the death of their white husbands. In these cases the children had an opportunity, which some of them took, to participate in Indian-oriented activities and to learn from their stepfather and his friends of Indian traditions. The two people I knew had learned the language and established recognized positions within the Indian-oriented society. They work with the Indians, dance with them, and often play a part in the rituals, yet, in balance, remain white-oriented in belief, values, and life-style. Such people are effective mediators between the two divisions and able interpreters of the Indian to the whites.

The experiences of many other mixed-blood families parallel in general those that I have described. They begin with the marriage of one white and one Indian parent who train their children to white ways. There are numerous variations in the details of subsequent marriages and experiences: children in the second generation frequently married mixed-blood spouses whose background was similar to their own instead of continuing a series of marriages to whites, as was done in the cases cited. The occupations chosen and the relative success or failure at these differed widely too. They share one basic element, however, over several generations the socialization patterns have been those of the dominant society and this has produced white-oriented tribal members.

Socialization to Indian-Orientation

The main avenue to present-day Indian-orientation has been the continuity of socialization to traditional ways modified by the attempts of the parents in each generation to cope with changing conditions and by each person's experiences with school, church, agency, and neighbors. Typical family histories are hard to find. Indian-oriented people were faced with many more options than the white-oriented. White-oriented families knew and were committed to the goals of financial independence; they were familiar with and supported what was taught in the schools and churches and knew what farming, ranching and business were all about. Most of the Indian-oriented, on the other hand, were from families where the things the parents and grandparents knew and understood did not fit the times. People in each generation learned bits and pieces of two traditions and had to learn which behavior, old or new, was appropriate depending on the circumstances. They were involved in the experiments with new subsistence techniques, in experiments that more often than not failed to produce a reliable and meaningful economic base for family and personal development. The following cases can only suggest some themes common to the backgrounds of the Indian-oriented people.

James Red Robe was born to full-blood parents in 1920. His childhood memories are of living in a cabin on Little Badger Creek, where his parents were raising potatoes, vegetables, chicken, and sheep under Agent Campbell's "Five Year Plan." He and his brothers and sisters were raised here and completed the eighth grade in the neighborhood school where they learned to speak and read English.

James' father, Harry Red Robe, and his mother were both born in 1890, and had lived through the trials of readaptation after the end of the buffalo days. Both parents became Catholics and had a few years of sporadic schooling, but gained most of their knowledge from what their own parents knew and taught them, plus what they learned by living through the years of change. Harry got his name when he was registered on the agency ration rolls. Here Red Robe found that the name he had paid an old medicine man to give his son was not important. The encounter with the agency roll clerk is not hard to imagine: Clerk to interpreter—"He is his son and a Christian. We have to give him a Christian surname. No one can pronounce the old man's name; what does it mean in English? Red Robe? All right tell him that his name is now Red Robe and his son will be called Harry Red Robe. We'll have to name the rest of the family too."

Harry tried and failed at farming and ranching in turn as many others did, but managed to keep his family alive and together with what he raised, supplemented by wage work on ranches, irrigation canal construction and by drawing rations when all else failed. The best days, according to James, were those that came after his father had quit ranching and devoted his time to raising horses, visiting, taking part in Indian social and ritual activities, interrupting these every now and then to work for the ranchers who were leasing his land. James remembers all the meetings, dances and ritual occasions. Both he and his father belonged to the Slick Feet, a society to which most of the men in the neighborhood, even a couple of white men, belonged. The "real" members, according to James, were the Indian men who had "paid" to get in. People came from all around when the society sponsored a dance. They camped along the creek, feasted, danced and had give-aways. "Everything was horses in those days, only a few people had cars. I can remember times when men brought unbroken horses right into the hall and gave them away."

James worked on his uncle's ranch and began to build a herd of his own using loan cattle. He was just getting a good start, he said, when he was called into the service during World War II. No one would care for his stock so he returned the loan cattle and sold the surplus. Since the war he has worked for wages at whatever he can find to do. He married a girl from a similar background. She works hard to raise their children and to maintain a home on what James brings in supplemented with what the older children can earn, help from kinsmen, and welfare payments during the winter.

James is Indian-oriented—he remembers and values what he learned about Indian ways from his parents and friends. He has been cured several times by an old man and has seen others cured as well. He has been present at bundle openings and participated in the Slick Feet rituals. "I didn't used to believe all that stuff, but after the cures I changed my mind." He insisted, however, that his children were good Catholics, and that he is the only one in his own family that still believes in some of the old Indian religion. I am unable to predict the orientation that will be taken by his children. He says that they do not speak Blackfeet and know nothing about the traditions. They do not take part in Indian social activities. On the other hand the people the children see most frequently are Indian-oriented and their own friends are the children of Indian-oriented families. James could give me no idea about what goals he had in mind for them.

Edward Chief's Son told a generally similar story except that his forebears had been among the leading families of Blackfeet society. His grandfather and father had managed to accumulate a little more, and build a larger following of kin and friends than Harry Red Robe had been able to do. Both of his grandfathers had been medicine men, bundle owners, and ritualists. None of them had been band chiefs, but had gained names as men of note within their bands.

Edward said that both of his parents were raised as Catholics and both had gone to about the fourth grade in school. They spoke some English but the Blackfeet language was used in the home while Edward and his brother and sisters were growing up. Edward told me little of his father's work experience. He was one of the "ranchers" who had ended up leasing his trust lands to other ranchers. The father, while nominally a Catholic, was also a bundle owner, curer, and ritualist who had sponsored a Sun Dance in which Edward and his brother had taken part. The children heard old stories, tales, and legends from their father and his friends during many an evening; they went with their parents to visit friends and relatives, to bundle openings, song services, and society dances. He learned to dance and sing and was taught much of the ritual. The father taught his children through story, example, and experience to appreciate Indian ways.

Edward has had more experience with the outside world than James. He served longer in the army and was sent overseas during World War II. He married soon after the war and has maintained his family on the lease money from his own and inherited trust lands, irregular wage labor on the reservation and, in past years, by traveling out of state with his family to work in the hop, apple, and potato harvests. In school he participated in sports and 4-H work, and he is presently an active member of the American Legion. He is a member and a leader in one of the Indian societies and frequently sings with one of the song groups.

This man is not much more secure financially than James, but he has more self-assurance and an established role among the Indian-oriented segment of the community. Some of the difference may stem from the relative social standing of their respective parents and the expectations that followed from this. Edward said, "I know I'm a full-blood and like to keep the old things alive." Unlike James, he teaches these things to his children and encourages them to learn to dance and to take part in Indian social activities. I would predict that they will be Indian-oriented when they grow up.

Raymond Black Plume's background was similar to that of Edward. He too is descended from leading men on both sides of the family, but he and others like him often appear to be younger children of large families who are singled out, for reasons not clear to me, for more education. It may be that they showed greater interest and could be allowed more time away from subsistence chores. Raymond did well in school, and completed high school where he was active in sports and Boy Scout work. One of his teachers took an interest in him and saw to it that he was included in several trips to West Coast cities. The teacher encouraged him to continue his education and helped him win a scholarship that supported him through one year of college. Raymond did not continue with college work, but he had acquired a proficiency in English and the social experience with white people than enables him to be an effective spokesman for the Indian-oriented group in the council and in national Indian organizations. Raymond, too, values his Indian heritage and, with the support of his wife, teaches his children the "best of the old and the best of the new."

The Indian-oriented group includes mixed-bloods too. Several people registered as ⅛, ¾, and ⅝ Blackfeet include an English or French trader or trapper in their genealogies. In these cases, however, whether married or not, the white grand- or great-grandparent either died or left his family when the children were very young. The mother returned to her family where she and her kinsmen raised the children in traditional ways. These children usually married full-bloods and socialized their children to be Indian-oriented. People with these backgrounds are essentially Indians who happen to have had a white grandfather or great-grandfather. The white man did not remain as a guide or model to teach his descendants anything about white culture.

Not all men and women from such backgrounds end up as Indian-oriented. At each generation there have been those who turned to the new and tended to forget or failed to learn much of Indian culture. Some left the reservation and became assimilated, some remained on the reservation as white-oriented, but many others who made such a break, often as they approached middle age, have either rejected the white world or felt rejected by it and returned to resume or relearn the old and now more highly valued Indian cultural patterns.

Analysis

These few examples of socialization experience leading to one or the other cultural orientation seem to show some common features. Parents teach their children what they know and believe. Where a parent was white-oriented and remained to direct the training of his children, or provided a teacher and model to the same end, the children tended to become white-oriented. Bruner (1956: 608–609) considered the presence of a "white model" to have been an important factor in the assimilation of the Mandan Indians. Where the experience of the parents, what they knew and believed, was from the Indian culture, this was transmitted to the children. Where the parents seem uncertain about what their children should be, as James now is, the next generation may be ill-prepared for a place in either group unless their peers, a teacher, or some elder provides a model or guidance that will give the children goals they now appear to lack.

These examples show, too, the complexity of the processes that underlie the present social diversity. The assimilation model held in the minds of administrators, priests, ministers, and teachers appears to have been one in which an Indian couple raised their children as Indians, the school and church changed or altered these children toward assimilation goals, and these upon becoming parents, moved their children even further toward that assimilation. Such a progression has occurred and some present tribal members are white-oriented because their family histories have followed such a course, but many other paths have been followed. Some tribal members are white-oriented because they were raised in families where there had been few or no traits of Indian culture to transmit, others had moved in one or two generations from Indian cultural backgrounds to a white-oriented life style and commitment. Other tribal members are Indian-oriented because members of their families have resisted assimilation, have sought to retain some things from the past even as they accepted some aspects of white culture. There are other

Indian-oriented people who had apparently rejected their cultural heritage but later in life came to value things that they had been exposed to during childhood and either learned or re-learned to be Indians again. There are those, too, among the Indian-oriented who have maintained the values and attitudes and a few of the practices learned in their childhood homes while at the same time learning to adapt to and even to use much from the white man's culture.

In this chapter I have suggested that there are two contrasting social groups living on the Blackfeet Indian reservation that differ significantly in their cultural orientations, and I have stressed that differing socialization patterns have been at work throughout the history of Blackfeet and white contact that maintained and perpetuated this division. One segment of the tribe has blocked or delayed assimilation forming an Indian-oriented society even as other tribal members moved toward assimilation and joined those who were born assimilated to form the white-oriented group. More of the content and direction of these differences in cultural transmission will become clear in the following discussion of the interaction patterns, values and status structures of the two divisions.

6

Social Interaction

Introduction

THE FOLLOWING ASSESSMENT of social interaction is based on observations made during the course of interviews, during attendance at group and community social gatherings, while visiting people in varying situations, and by observing people in stores and on the street. In addition, much information was gleaned from comments of informants and from the local weekly newspaper.

The original orientation categories used reported interest or participation in some social activities as defining criteria; the concern now is to show that these people actually did attend and participate in these affairs but did not take part in others. Then other forms of social gathering for which I have data are discussed to further support the contention that people of each orientation interact more frequently among themselves than they do with people of the other orientation.

As my fieldwork progressed, the impression grew that in some situations people of both orientations participated in relatively equal numbers; in other contexts the Indian-oriented people formed the majority in attendance, while other social gatherings attracted mainly white-oriented persons. The three types of social gatherings are discussed separately and in that order.

Social Occasions Where Everybody Came

Both Indian- and white-oriented people were noted at political rallies, tribal council meetings, church, sports events, and rodeos. Other situations where relatively equal participation between people of both orientations was noticeable were in business and work contexts where the relationships were those of buyer-seller, service-client, and employee-employer.

Council meetings draw people from all segments of the tribe, as it is at these meetings that issues of interest to all are discussed. The largest crowds turn out when meetings are held to vote on per capita payments, or decisions about the use of Indian land are being considered. At such meetings people of both orientations are present and are equally vocal in support of or in opposition to proposals made. Both orientation groups are represented in the council. At meetings I attended, one or two old timers used the time prior to the opening of the meeting to make speeches, loudly haranguing the usually inattentive audience about the problems of the full-bloods. Council minutes frequently record the speeches of the Honorary Councilmen, who contribute to the debate, such as the translation of a speech recorded several years back in which an honored elder spoke about procedures in preparing a land claim case against the U.S. government:

> I am speaking to all of you my people. We have the time and we have the chance to discuss the true evidence that we have and we should use them for our discussions. Don't use things that will puzzle up our claims. Use the facts to determine your progress. In my memory there was a time when a claim matter came up and several members of the tribe tried to use evidence that was not right. I told them to bring out only the true facts and if they were presented with our faith in them we would be sure to win our case. I believe that if we proceed according to treaties and agreements made with the government we will make some progress on our claims. Let's work with the chosen leaders of our tribe. I'm sure they are doing the best they can for us . . . (Unpublished documents of the Blackfeet Tribal Council).

Campaign meetings are held in Browning and the outlying communities preceding each biennial election of tribal councilmen. As many as sixty-five to seventy candidates run for office, and most of them attend these meetings to explain their stands on political issues, and to solicit voter support at the polls. Most of the meetings I attended in Browning took place in a centrally located building where the attendance was mixed. The orientation differences were recognized, however, by arranging other meetings at the homes of some of the "full-bloods" where Indian-oriented people were most numerous of those attending. Attendance at meetings in the outlying communities is proportionate to the composition of the community population; that is, Starr School and Heart Butte have a larger proportion of Indian-oriented present than at similar meetings at Babb or East Glacier where the population is more balanced or even largely white-oriented.

The political meetings draw interested people from both segments of the reservation population because the issues discussed affect the affairs of all. All candidates at meetings I attended made some allusion to their own Indian identification, that is, "we Indians," "the white man is after our land and we Indians must prevent this." Speeches emphasized the need to stop white encroachment, the imminence and dangers of termination, the need to preserve the land base. Calls were made for better education, more jobs, more per capita payments and better management of tribal funds. Some candidates spoke in English, others in Blackfeet, and the speeches of both were translated into the other language by an interpreter. I was impressed by the fairness of the interpretation. Often the translator was a candidate himself, yet he translated objectively the remarks of the other speakers, occasionally turned a haltingly given speech into a forceful and dynamic one, and included remarks that were critical of his own candidacy, or performance in office. On one occasion the interpreter gave introductory recognition to candidates who were unable to attend and commented that "your support at the polls would be most appreciated" by those candidates. People running for office draw upon ties of kinship that might have been overlooked or ignored in the recent past. It is often said that if you can get the support of a few key people you can be assured of the "full-blood vote," indicating the belief that kinsmen will vote with their family leaders.

People of both orientations attend church services according to individual interests and needs. Leaders of the different denominations actively proselyte among both unaffiliated people and the membership of the other churches. Interest in church attendance appears to follow the patterns indicated in the responses to my questionnaire where only three of the Indian-oriented and four of the white-oriented reported regular church attendance.

Rodeos and sports events are occasions for the largest gatherings which include relatively equal attendance and participation by people of both orientations. The rodeo attracts the largest crowds. These are public events open to all who buy a ticket and are given wide publicity; the participants are largely local people and drawn from both orientation groups.

People from both groups were seen in attendance at rodeos held in Browning and at Birch Creek during each summer of fieldwork. The informal grouping in the stands and around the grounds appear to be based on family and friendship ties. Families—parents, children and grandchildren—sit together. People apart from their families sit with their friends. In the rural areas, the spectators sit in cars and trucks, or stand around the arena. They cheer for their kinsmen and friends and jeer at the opposition; it is a lively and often moving crowd. Cultural orientations appear to operate in the smaller groupings that make up the larger crowds.

The sports events draw smaller numbers of people than do the rodeos, but the nature of participation and attendance is similar. One such event, an elementary school track meet I attended, appeared particularly noteworthy because it is comparable in many respects to the Easter Egg Hunt described later in this section.

This track and field meet between the Browning and neighborhood elementary schools was an activity in which children took part without regard to the orientation of their families. It was held at the Browning High School track on a cold, blustery spring day and people of both orientations attended—parents, teachers, and track fans. Informal groupings by family and friends were noted here too, but it was a moving crowd and interaction patterns were hard to identify.

Various other public ceremonies attract participants and on-lookers from all segments of the population, usually on the basis of who has an interest in the particular event scheduled. I recall two such occasions: a ceremony honoring an Air Force contingent from Malmstrom Air Force Base near Great Falls in 1959 and the dedication of a War Veterans memorial by the War Mothers on the grounds of the Museum of the Plains Indian in 1967. Both ceremonies were held on the Museum grounds and drew participants from both orientations—Tribal Councilmen, Honorary Councilmen, the American Legion Color Guard, and in the latter ceremony, the War Mothers and families of veterans who had died in action.

The Air Force ceremony struck several of us as a test of the time sense of two cultures. Two Air Force generals were to be honored by being given a Blackfeet name and honorary membership in the Blackfeet tribe. The ritual called for a speech by an elderly chief at the conclusion of which he would pronounce the name he was giving the general, and place a war bonnet on the head of the newly adopted tribesman. A second chief would then make the bestowal to the other general. Air Force plans called for a jet plane fly-over as the war bonnet was put on the head of the senior officer. Four members of the Honorary Council, the master of ceremonies and an interpreter, dressed in Indian regalia, stood in an informal group at one side awaiting the beginning of the ceremonies, while to the other an Air Force contingent consisting of the two generals, fifteen full colonels and a captain, and a color guard of a sergeant and five enlisted men, were drawn up in formation. There was much synchronizing of watches on the military side, a relaxed unconcerned waiting on the part of the Blackfeet. The jets were evidently airborne somewhere over the horizon; if there was radio communication between the planes and the group on the ground, I did not see it.

The ceremony began. Air Force participation could be and was done according to a planned time sequence, but no one could predict how long one of the chiefs might choose to speak. Yet even as I was figuring the odds on outcome, the old chief concluded his speech and pronounced the name, the interpreter translated it, the war bonnet went up and the jets came over the horizon, over the group on the ground and out of sight in the direction of Great Falls. Someone, I will never know who, had good medicine.

The War Memorial dedication was a concern of local people and brought together an audience of families of veterans and tribal dignitaries. It marked the success of a drive begun many years earlier by the War Mothers (mothers of war veterans) to raise money for such a memorial, so commemorated too their persistence and hard work. A procession of tribal leaders, some in Indian regalia, the American Legion Color Guard, the Boy Scouts, and the War Mothers was followed by speeches from the Gold Star Mothers and the unveiling of the pylon shaped monument upon which was mounted a bronze plaque inscribed with the names of tribal members who had been killed in action in U.S. wars. Later in the day the War Mothers staged a give-away ceremony in memory of these war dead.

Indian-Oriented Social Occasions

The social occasions where most of the participants and spectators are people of Indian orientation include several public, semiprivate and private gatherings. Some are formal occasions while others are informal in their organization. Formal public occasions include the North American Indian Days celebrations at Browning, a Sun Dance held in conjunction with one of these, and periodically scheduled Indian dances. Horse races and stick game gatherings in the outlying communities are frequent forms of public entertainment organized on a less formal basis. The private and semiprivate gatherings are those to which attendance is invited, tacitly or directly, and some of the formal occasions for such congregation are medicine bundle openings, curing ceremonies, song services, and private parties. House to house visiting, gatherings of families and friends, the visiting grouping at the formal public activities, in office buildings and stores, and street corner visiting are kinds of informal private interaction.

The Indian Days celebrations are annual affairs sponsored by the reservation community. The tribal council makes an appropriation to underwrite the celebration, and local businessmen make cash contributions or put up prizes for competitive events. The four day celebration, held in late June or early July, is a reenactment of the traditional Blackfeet summer encampment and advertised widely as a tourist attraction. Families who own tepees are encouraged to pitch them on the encampment grounds and to camp there with their families. Indians from other reservations are invited, resulting in a camp circle of fifty or more tepees formed by local people, visitors from the Canadian Reserves—Blood, North Piegan, Blackfoot and Cree—and from surrounding United States Indian communities—Warm Springs, Yakima, Umatilla, Crow, Gros Ventre, Cheyenne, Assiniboine, Flathead, and Cree, among others. Sleeping and cooking tents are erected behind the tepee circle and upwards of seven hundred people live on the grounds during the encampment. Each family camping on the grounds is paid a cash allowance toward their maintenance and shares in a daily meat or food ration.

The formal program opens with a parade through the main street of Browning and out to the encampment grounds near the Museum of the Plains Indian, a half mile west of town. A regular program of Indian dancing to the accompaniment of singing and drumming by local and visiting singing groups is scheduled each afternoon, and continues long into the evening if the weather permits.

The dancing sessions are interrupted frequently by both planned and unplanned intermission activities—special dance contests, games, and "give-aways." Some of the last mentioned gift giving ceremonies are sponsored by the Indian Days Committee to honor and give gifts to invited guests from other tribes. Others are put on by individuals and families who wish—and are expected—to give gifts in remembrance of a deceased relative, to give a new and significant Indian name to a child in a public naming ceremony, or to honor some other person by a display of generosity in his name. The person to be honored and his family form a procession and pass four times around the dance arena as the singers drum and sing a favored song. A similar procession is formed for the memorial give-away, and a close relative carries a photograph of the deceased relative. Increasingly distant relatives join the procession with each turn. Quantities of gifts are brought in and at the conclusion of the processional, a crier acting for the family calls out the names of those to be given gifts. Occasionally a tepee with furnishings is given, sometimes horses, more usually blankets, cigarettes, and cash make up the gifts.

Another almost regularly occurring part of the program is a ceremony in which distinguished visitors are adopted into the Blackfeet Tribe. These people are given an Indian name and a war bonnet, or other tokens of their new status, by an honored elder. In 1960, Indian Days coincided with the U.S. Governors

Conference at Many Glaciers Lodge in Glacier National Park. Six of the governors who visited the encampment were honored by adoption and given names, and the Governor of Virginia was selected to respond for the others. He began by remarking that the people of Virginia felt a special and warm regard for the Indians. "If it had not been for the help of the Indians the Jamestown settlement would not have survived that first winter." A Blackfeet standing beside me gave me a dig in the ribs with his elbow and said, "that's the day we lost the war."

The encampment also provides the opportunity for other forms of social expression. Medicine bundles are opened with attendant prayers, dances, and face-painting. Men may be "captured" to become members of the Dog society, an honor that must be paid for in goods or cash. People visit from tepee to tepee, drink coffee, eat, and talk. Sometimes one or more of the elderly Indian-oriented leaders will provide a lunch of boiled beef, bread, salad, doughnuts, cookies, cake, and coffee to all who wish to come.

By midafternoon a stick game or two gets under way near one of the concesion booths behind the tent area and usually continues until dawn. Sometimes known as the "hand game," this is a popular and widely known Indian gambling game. All that is required is space, two poles, planks, or timbers placed about three feet apart parallel to each other, two "bones," or short wooden cylinders about ½ inch in diameter and two inches long, one banded and the other plain, and some plain sticks about ten to twelve inches long, usually ten to a side to use as markers. Two teams line up facing each other behind each pole. One person starts the game by intently shuffling, showing, and after many flourishes hiding the bones, one in each hand. His team chants and drums with sticks on the pole in front of them to give him support and to confuse the opposition during the hiding. Finally he extends his hands so that one of the players on the other side can choose by one of several signs which hand holds the unmarked bone. If the "guesser" fails to choose correctly, his side forfeits one of their marker sticks and the "hider" tries again; if he guesses correctly, the bones and roles change sides. The game is over when one side wins all of the marker sticks. Bets between individuals, both participants and onlookers, are placed before the game begins and other bets are made frequently on the results of individual guesses. There are many variations in the procedure that I have not mastered. A bettor gets a lot of action for his money whether he fully understands what is happening or not. The drumming, chanting, joking, as well as the strain of waiting for the outcome of a game in which large sums of money are at stake, contribute to an exciting time.

People spend the rest of the time during the encampment doing the necessary chores of camp living and enjoying the pastimes appropriate to sex and age—the children play games, older people work on costumes, play blackjack, visit, loaf, or go into town.

In spite of this being a community enterprise with fairly large crowds that are attracted to it, the people in relatively continuous attendance are the Indian-oriented. The people who camp on the grounds and participate in the festivities include and appear to be like the men I interviewed and classed as Indian-oriented. In retrospect, I would sort the onlookers into four categories: (a) Indian-oriented spectators from many parts of the reservation who spend much time on the grounds and can be seen in attendance day after day, (b) a number of people recognized as of white-orientation who make a brief appearance, spend an hour or two watching the proceedings and then leave, (c) a few white-oriented people, who because of special community roles and interests have reason to be in attendance more frequently, and (d) a changing tourist attendance of twenty-five to one hundred persons who spend varying amounts of time enjoying the spectacle. The patterns of attendance and participation appear to be changing. During the past ten years, many older people have died and fewer expert ritualists are left, but younger people are getting involved in the dancing. In 1959, I noted that few teenagers were dancing; the dancers tended to be either over thirty or under twelve years old. In 1970, these youngsters had become teenagers and were still turning out. More children were dancing. All age ranges seemed to be represented. In addition, several children from white-oriented families were seen to be buying costumes and learning to dance.[12]

The most recent Sun Dances were performed in 1959 and 1964 and the ceremony I observed (1959) was held in conjunction with that year's Indian Days. The religious ceremonies were held on the encampment grounds preceding the secular festivities. A "Medicine Lodge" was constructed with appropriate ritual by setting up a circle of ten poles around a center post: rafters were strung between these poles and from each pole to the center post and lashed into place with strips of hide. An opening was left to the east, and the wall and "roof" at the west end were covered with leafy cottonwood branches to make a sun and wind shelter for the ritualists who worked inside. The participants were largely people of Indian-orientation as were most of the spectators. Modern Indian-orientation does not require full knowledge and belief in the old religion. While the key roles were filled by older men who knew the ritual, other people were chosen more because they came close to the model of "good Indian people" than for their knowledge of the ritual. Some others were selected because they were kin of the more traditional participants or were among the social and political leaders from both segments of the community. One woman told me that she had been "captured" and had paid for the privilege of "owning" the knife and the right to cut the hide into strips for the lashings on the Medicine Lodge. This was traditionally a male prerogative, and in this case a male relative acted for her. In 1964 a young man conducted the ritual, thus assuming a role usually reserved for an older man. He had been trained from childhood by his grandfather and other elders, so perhaps was better qualified in this respect than most living elders, but his action appeared to have made some of the older people uneasy. Such changes aside, the ceremonies are solemn, the key participants are involved in rituals that have deep meaning for them; the other participants pay respect to the beliefs expressed, and the families and friends of the people involved watch the proceedings with mixed emotions of interest, understanding, tolerance and respect.

Social dancing at the Indian Days Celebration functions as both entertainment for the tourists and recreation for the participants. The dancers do not

---

[12] Participation by these young people might introduce some confusion into my orientation schemes, but for reasons I will discuss in the final chapter, I think that their participation does not signal a turn toward Indian-orientation on their part.

await an audience but start dancing when they feel like it, often whenever a sing-ing group begins to drum. The entertainment rarely follows the schedule, but starts and stops according to the mood of the individual dancers. Some arrive on time, others an hour or two late. Evening dances are or are not held depending upon the weather and the inclination of the dancers, rather than upon the presence of an audience. In fact many dancers show signs of impatience with the tourist onlookers who often invade the dance circle to take pictures. Tourists appear to be a tolerated nuisance rather than spectators to be entertained. The Indian visitors, who understand the dancing and participate at least vicariously, are the more orderly, appreciative and appreciated audience. The point is that the dancing at the encampment is a social and recreational outlet, and for the people involved it is an experience that plays a very important and meaningful part in their lives. During these days they are "Indians," doing things that symbolized this identity. They stress social positions of importance among "Indians" that may have little relation to the world at large. People have a special competence here that is recog-nized by their peers.

People who own dancing costumes leave the reservation frequently during the summer and fall to participate in similar Indian gatherings held throughout the plains area. Indian-oriented families may be gone for most of the summer, and the anthropologist who stays behind knows that he is missing out on events that are an important part of the lives of these people.

In the late fall, winter, and early spring a series of social dances, often coinciding with national holidays, are held at the community halls in surrounding neighborhoods. People from other parts of the reservation are invited or are free to attend. Often people came from neighboring reservations as well.

These dances, at the Heart Butte, Starr School, or other community houses, are usually sponsored by one of the men's societies. Those I attended in the spring of 1960 were scheduled for an early evening start, yet it was usually around nine o'clock before the dancing began. The Grass and Fancy dancers were in costume and Grass, War, and other dances by those in costume were mixed with Owl dances—round dances for men and women partners—in which all could partici-pate whether in costume or not. Here, as in the Indian Days program, time was taken for give-aways—at least one was put on by the sponsoring society to honor guests and others were put on by individuals for varying reasons. At midnight the wives, sisters, and daughters of the sponsoring society members served a lunch to all in attendance, then dancing was resumed to continue until dawn. Newspaper and informants' reports indicated that the dances I attended were typical and that they continue to be held.

The attendance and participation at these dances confirmed the reports from my sample; those I identified as Indian-oriented were present, while few of the white-oriented people turned out. The crowds (usually estimated from three to four hundred in number) were made up of the same people who had been seen in most constant attendance at the Indian Days programs.

The more Indian-oriented communities of Starr School and Heart Butte alternately sponsor horse racing in their neighborhoods almost weekly during the

A round dance for couples—everybody is invited to dance whether in costume or not.

A give-away ceremony.

summer and fall. Horse owners and racing fans from many parts of the reservation turn out to visit and watch the horses run. Interregional rivalry is often intense. The fastest horses become well-known so the outcome of the races often turns on the weight and ability of the jockey and the possibility of gaining an advantage at the start. Much time is spent in getting the betting arranged, so that two or three races are about all that can be run in an afternoon.

Stick games are often played after the races, and at Heart Butte the games are a regular part of the year-around weekend activities. A public room arranged for playing the stick game as well as pool and cards was a regular gathering place for the people of Heart Butte until it burned down a few years ago. The weekly stick games have moved to a new location on Badger Creek.

The horse races attract some white-oriented horse fans, but the majority of the crowd is Indian-oriented. Races are occasions for Indian rivalry and above all to enjoy each other's company. The stick games have a regular but more limited following and with few exceptions, players and observers are Indian-oriented.

Song services are meetings of the singing groups and serve both as practice sessions and as forms of social gathering for the people involved. The sessions are uually held in the home of one of the singers, a relative, or a friend. A few kinsmen and friends—young and old, men and women—attend and the evening is spent in singing and drumming old and new songs. The sessions break up at the discretion of the singers and may be followed by a late supper.

Bundle openings and curing ceremonies (according to informant and newspaper reports) are religious rituals to which guests are invited. The reports indicate that those in attendance are always people of Indian-orientation. Some are believers and others are sympathetic but noncommitted members of the participants' families. The activities on these occasions are determined by the ritual of the particular bundle or cure, but involve singing, drumming, prayers and some dancing by selected participants. The owner of the bundle regularly paints the faces of those in attendance as a mark of prayer for their well being. Bundle opening ceremonies are followed by a feast. One such ceremony held at Starr School was described by one of the neighbors:

> The beaver dance given by Jim White Calf was held at the home of Jim and Amy Whitegrass despite the terrific storm and sudden cold. There were many people from Browning out to see this rare dance, that has long been forgotten. Among those attending were Mr. and Mrs. Fish Wolf Robe, Mr. and Mrs. Charlie Horn, Mr. and Mrs. Tom Many Guns and Mary Ground besides the many people of our community. The dance began with the rythmic [sic] beating on hides to certain songs. The bundle was opened by Jim White Calf and Maggie Many Hides. The bundle consists of many skins of useful animals and small birds that are of help to the owner. The beaver for "energy," the otter for "speed," the ermine for "beauty," the swan for "grace" and the little birds for their endurance of the cold in the winter. The people were then painted and eight danced in a most graceful manner. Maggie Many Hides, Mary Ground, Isabelle, Cecile Horn, Mrs. Fish, Annie Old Person, Mrs. Tom Many Guns all danced like beavers with sticks in their mouths and hands. The usual meal was served after a monstrous amount of energy was put into the dancing and singing. A delicious berry soup, boiled meat, fried bread and a dessert were consumed by everyone. At the end of the dance one certain lady gets up and dances with little small deer hooves and punches a man in the crowd and it goes on until everyone is dancing. It was a most enjoyable occasion for a grand time was had by all (*Glacier Reporter*, October 12, 1961:6).

This "dance" was "long forgotten" by the reporter and others in the community but not by the bundle-owner and the named participants, several of whom owned or had owned bundles themselves. Here was a gathering of Indian-oriented people conducting an Indian ceremony. Some undoubtedly experienced the deep religious experience of a beaver bundle opening, others had a "grand time" at a "most enjoyable occasion," a social gathering of people who shared interests in aspects of Indian culture.

The social grouping of Indian-oriented people gains further support from observations of informal clustering. At the Indian Days encampment, and at the social dances in particular, it was relatively easy to watch for the Indian-oriented people and to notice with whom they spent their time in informal groupings— visiting, chatting, watching, and relaxing. Most of such visiting was with people of similar orientation with only occasional mixing among men of differing orienta-

The forming of the tepee circle for North American Indian Days.

tions. Other observations and reports further support these conclusions. Visits to homes, reported visiting among families and friends, and observations of grouping on other occasions reinforced the pattern.

In 1962 I wrote:

> Perhaps the most visible visiting pattern for the Indian-oriented people is the very regular daily congregation in sidewalk groups. From late spring to mid-autumn as many as eighty people can be seen standing or sitting at fairly pre-dictable locations around the town. The location is determined by people's inclinations and by the requirements of sun, shade, or shelter from the wind. People pass many hours a day, visiting and watching the passers-by. White-oriented men are on the street but stop for only short periods of time and then move on, but the Indian-oriented man and his friends make this a major avocation.
>
> If the weather is bad the visitors form smaller groups and move into the nearby

buildings for shorter periods of time. Most of the men, if asked or if they happen to volunteer the information, have a reason for being there. They are available if someone should be looking for a hired hand; they are waiting for the mail, or keeping an appointment. Sometimes this is true but a comparison of the time spent with the chores accomplished strongly indicates that visiting with friends and watching the town activities with them, are the important objectives (McFee 1962:141).

There have been changes in these patterns since that time. Some businesses have moved to other parts of town diluting the concentration of occupied buildings in the central section, and the people have shifted too. Groups are smaller and scattered. The two grocery stores still serve as gathering places, the new Community Center and Tribal Office Building, located south of town and near much of the new low rent and mutual aid housing development, will undoubtedly provide a new focus for informal visiting groups and draw them further from the center of town. These patterns too will change but this form of visiting will continue. There is little else to do between infrequent jobs, and money is scarce. Some people will move into the bars when they have money, but there is a limit on how much time and money can be spent there. Others have no interest in the bars anyway. So men and women pass the time with the street corner groups or wander off to continue visiting in cars or at one another's homes.

Indian-oriented people appear to spend more time in social interaction with people of similar orientation than with others. It was to be expected from the way Indian orientation was defined, that people of this category would participate in the social activities that have been described. An examination of the limited participation by these people in other reservation social activities makes the social unity of this group more apparent.

White-Oriented Social Occasions

The areas of predominantly white-oriented interaction are again both public and private. The public social gatherings that I observed were most frequently centered around school and civic service themes and included P.T.A. meetings, school programs, commencement exercises, Youth Club activities, children's Fishing Derbies, and an annual Easter Egg Hunt. Other activities, such as bowling tournaments and civic club meetings, are of a semiprivate nature in that there is selective membership. The private occasions, as with the Indian-oriented group, would include parties, picnics, and visiting.

There appear to be no large community enterprises that draw crowds of white-oriented people together comparable to the Indian Days Encampment and the Indian dances around which so much Indian-oriented sociability is focused. Perhaps the unbalanced attendance at school and civic meetings—activities involving the children of the community—is most striking and comparable. The limited adult attendance at these events indicates a real social division within the community that can be explained, in part, by the cultural orientations.

School plays, commencement exercises, and the other child and youth activities in Browning invite public support.[13] Children from families of both orientations attend and participate; yet very few of the parents who turn out to watch their children perform are Indian-oriented.

The P.T.A. meetings and school commencement exercises I went to were not attended by many Indian-oriented people. No Indian-oriented were seen at two P.T.A. meetings, each attended by from fifty to sixty people. In 1960, twenty-one (over a third) of an eighth grade graduating class of sixty-seven were from identifiable Indian families, yet few Indian-oriented adults were in the audience.

The high school commencement held on the evening of the same day, differed considerably in the nature of attendance. In this instance a class of thirty-three graduating seniors included twenty-five tribal members. Eight of this number (approximately a fourth) could be identified as children from Indian-oriented families. The proportion of Indian-oriented among the seniors was smaller than for the eighth grade class, but more Indian-oriented adults were at the high school commencement, making up an estimated fifth of the audience. Even so, the largest part of those in attendance were white-oriented. Even smaller Indian-oriented attendance was reported for the preceding and following graduations.

The larger Indian attendance in 1960 may have been because the valedictorian was a full-blood boy. I had seen him dancing at the Indian social dances and at the Indian Days Celebrations, and on these occasions he wore a beaded buckskin suit that he had made and decorated himself. He was one of a very few young men who wore their hair in braids. Perhaps some of the Indian-oriented came to the commencement to see an Indian-oriented boy graduate with honors.

Attendance at the annual Easter Egg Hunts and the Fishing Derbies is more indicative. While these affairs are not comparable to an Indian Days Celebration, they are community sponsored, scheduled, recurrent and locally advertised. Children participate regardless of the orientation of their families. Perhaps these events and the previously described track meet are most comparable and the differences in attendance at each most revealing. In short, Indian-oriented parents attended the track meet but did not respond in the same way to the Egg Hunt and Fishing Derbies.

I observed the Easter Egg Hunt of 1960 and arrived too late for this event in following years. As usual it was held in an open field behind the Museum of the Plains Indian on the afternoon of Easter Sunday. The weather was much the same as it was for the track meet held one month later—cold and windy. Approximately five hundred children, from Indian, white, and white-oriented families took part. Children from the Cut Bank Boarding Dormitory were brought

---

[13] The description of these particular events is restricted to those held in Browning because it is the largest and most heterogeneous of the reservation communities. People of both orientations, local people and residents from the other communities, come to Browning to attend events that interest them. Attendance at similar affairs in outlying communities reflects the orientation balance of the community. Children's activities at Starr School and Heart Butte, for instance, are attended by more Indian-oriented people; similar events at Babb or East Glacier are attended almost wholly by white-oriented persons. Browning differs in that it has quite large populations of people from both orientations; selective turnout here is more significant.

in by bus; children from Starr School and other nearby neighborhoods came in cars driven by a teacher or parent to join in the search with the youngsters of Browning.

Members of the Browning Youth Club and the American Legion had distributed quantities of eggs, which had been boiled and colored by school children, in the furrows and stubble of the forty acre field. Some of the eggs were marked and cash awards were given to the finders of the special eggs. Prizes, donated by service clubs and local merchants, were given also for the most eggs collected by one child and to the runners-up.

This was a large area and people arrived at irregular intervals. Many watched from their cars, others moved about the periphery of the field, making an accurate count of the adults difficult, but it was apparent that the majority of those present were white and white-oriented people. Indian-oriented parents were few and even the Indian-oriented political leaders were absent.

The Fishing Derbies I witnessed drew a much smaller crowd, approximately two hundred children and sixty adults. The contests are held at a small lake adjacent to U.S. Route 2 a few miles southwest of Browning. The children fish along the shore, while the parents help with putting on bait and removing the fish that are caught. They cheer the children on, visit with each other, set up picnics, and eat. Everybody has a good time when a Fishing Derby is sponsored. An estimated third of the children taking part in these contests were from Indian-oriented families, yet only four or five Indian-oriented adults were in attendance.

In the realm of semiprivate interaction are included civic club meetings and bowling tournaments. The informants and the newspaper reports indicate an almost completely white-oriented participation in these activities.

Civic club membership is selective and based upon business, school, or political leadership. The selection factors are many and complex but it is clear that very few Indian-oriented people belong to these organizations—these are areas of predominantly white-oriented interaction.

Newspaper reports indicate that selective factors operate to maintain a predominantly white and white-oriented participation, particularly in team and tournament play, at the bowling alley. Factors of social selection also work in private gatherings and visiting patterns between families and friends. The bonds of kinship draw some of the Indian-oriented into the visiting patterns of white-oriented people, but these occasions are infrequent. Economic and status factors also appear to be important determinants of Indian-oriented participation in private activities.

Other Social Expressions of Orientation

The social division of the community that I am describing is given overt, but inexact, recognition by the use of the labels—"mixed-blood" and "full-blood." These "racial" stereotypes are used in many contexts but in most cases point up a division in culture that is only partially related to the number of Indian ancestors of any individual.

Ewers remarked on the rapid hybridization of the tribe and the decreasing numbers of full-bloods, and he noted the tendency for the latter to consider themselves to be "the real Blackfoot Indians—the true descendants of the great warriors and wise leaders of old and the preservers of all that is left of Blackfoot Indian culture" (Ewers 1958:328). According to the stereotype, the full-blood is conservative and the mixed-blood progressive. The surnames of the people still further label the difference—an English, French, or American name implies mixed genetic heritage, while the Indian name (in its agency recorded translation) is a badge of Indian heritage.

There are some grounds to support a popular notion of spatial separation of the two groups. Generally the lands north of Browning are thought to be mixed-blood territory and the full-bloods claim the southern part of the reservation. Recent migrations of people have upset this balance but the idea lingers on as an element in social separation. An increasing community feeling among concentrations of full-bloods at Starr School and Heart Butte, and some spatial clustering in Browning, is tending to replace the old regional division. Mixed marriages and shifting populations, however, are breaking down even these full-blood strongholds.

The full-blood-mixed-blood distinction is not equivalent to my categories of Indian and white orientations. Of the eight Indian-oriented men in my sample, only four are full-bloods, while one full-blood is categorized among the twenty white-oriented people. But the popular full-blood and mixed-blood labels gain some validity when it is noted that the Indian-oriented of the sample are all 3/4 or more Indian, while the white-oriented men are, with the one exception, 5/8 or less.

Such stereotypes produce conflicts. A series of statements by informants illustrate the mechanisms of social distance that appear to be important in limiting close social interaction between people of the two orientation groups.

For example, "Full-bloods hate mixed-bloods. They are tainted with the blood of those who robbed and ruined the Indian."

An informant overheard a mixed-blood girl complain, "They [full-bloods] are to blame. In the old days when things were bad they sold their daughters to the white men. Now they hate us."

A mixed-blood man said, "Full-bloods hate the mixed-bloods and would like to run them off the reservation. They get confused when I ask them, How about that white son-in-law of yours and your grandchildren? They finally decided that those were all right."

One man observed that little social distinction is felt by the children until they reach the upper grades. Then the more Indian children develop feelings of inferiority and inadequacy and drop out of school. "Much of the school problem is social," he said, "You see a bunch of grade school kids playing, mixed white and Indian, and you stop and ask them who is white and who is Indian? They just stare at you. The question doesn't make sense. At high school things begin to show up. Mostly social. The kids begin to want to invite each other to affairs at home. They begin to notice that they haven't the kind of clothes others do. They begin to feel they can't participate and drop out."

A recent high school graduate (mixed-blood, white-oriented) could offer no explanation of full-blood problems in the schools, either scholastic or social.

He neither knew what the "Indian" boys in his class did or thought, nor could he say what had caused others he had known in the lower grades to drop out. His father (mixed-blood, businessman and active in community service) explained this: "He doesn't go around with those fellows."

"The full-bloods are forgotten. The half-breeds up north are running things for their own benefit."—a full-blood.

"Full-bloods probably expect to be discriminated against. They realize that they are in a different class, so act that way and so are discriminated against. They tend to stay by themselves."—a mixed-blood.

"There is conflict between the full-bloods and the 'breeds.' The latter are more progressive. They try to push things the old folks don't understand. It's not a caste division, just a mistrust of methods and plans."—a full-blood.

Numerous factors are at work here—historical, economic, political and cultural. The elements of status and values that underlie these attitudes will be examined further in the following chapters. The accounts are offered here to indicate that a bicultural division is recognized by the people themselves, that the two groups have been stereotyped and labeled, and that both spatial and social separation have been attributed to these groups. One consequence has been a curtailment of social interaction between members of the two societies.

The concepts of cultural orientation cannot be confused with the stereotypes. The real division is cultural. Orientational differences however tend to produce behaviors frequently attributed to the stereotype. "Full-blood" behavior in many dimensions is the behavior of an Indian-oriented person. People who are Indian-oriented, regardless of genetic heritage or degree of acculturation toward American life, will adopt practices that others attribute to "Indians." Then too it must be remembered that orientations are not indelible labels to apply to individuals, but rather are indicative of social structure. They stand for social categories for which there are predictable behavioral expectations, norms, and underlying values. Individuals can move from one category to another by conforming to the proper set of norms and expressing the values common to that category. The degree of Indian "blood" does not "tell."

Summary

I have tried to show that the Indian-oriented and white-oriented people engage in social interaction most frequently with members of their own group. A series of public, formal and informal, social situations was reviewed, some of which were attended predominantly by Indian-oriented people, others by white. Another list of public gatherings was given in which attendance from the two groups was relatively equal. It was shown further that informal grouping at these affairs tended to be with people of like orientation. An additional tendency for limitations upon intergroup sociality was observed in informal and private entertaining and visiting, and the overt recognition of this social separation was commented upon.

The key to these attendance patterns seems to lie in the kinds of social affairs that attract the Indian audience. Where the social activity contains some symbol of Indian-ness, the Indian-oriented turn out. The Indian Days Celebration, the Indian social dances, bundle openings, stick games, and song services are highly symbolic to the Indian. Consequently, the attendance at these is mainly Indian-oriented. Conversely, white-oriented interest is minimal.

Where the occasions lack continuity with Indian interests, or lack some symbolic aspect for Indian identification, the Indian-oriented fail to participate. In the areas of sociality where mixed audiences were reported, some Indian identification symbols can be recognized. The rodeo, for instance, is directly related to past Indian experience with horses and with cattle raising—a form of white economic activity at which the Indian has achieved some success.

Sports events, too, carry some of the flavor of racing, physical activity and prowess from the past, and again, and probably of more significance, these are areas in which the Indian has been able to achieve a success recognized as such by the members of the dominant society. When viewed in this light, the Easter Egg Hunt stands in sharp contrast to the children's track meet. Sports are given Indian recognition while an Egg Hunt symbolizes nothing Indian. Indian-oriented people turn out to watch their children compete in the track meet but not at the Egg Hunt.

The high school commencement appeared to attract more Indian-oriented persons than did the eighth grade graduation program, but this may be because the high school valedictorian was an Indian. He was a symbol of Indian success in a white man's game, and it was success by an Indian who practiced Indian ways.

The observed interaction patterns indicate that there are separate social groups. Examination of the values and status systems will further substantiate this relationship and give additional insight into the reasons behind the kinds of participation in community and private social affairs.

7

Values

Introduction

TWO AGGREGATES OF PEOPLE each of which shares distinctive patterns of sociocultural characteristics have been identified as Indian-oriented and white-oriented, and evidence has been offered to show that the people within each category associate more frequently with each other than with people of the other orientation. If these are more than just aggregates of people with similar interests, however, it is necessary to show that each has the *esprit de corps* that Linton called the motivating power of a society (Linton 1936:107). This power can be found in the goals and related value judgments of each group, and these are examined in this chapter to see if contrast can be found in the value patterns of the categories.

People judge and evaluate the behavior of others on the basis of shared goals or purposes that follow from the premises they hold about the nature of man and the world and these premises influence how they raise their children. Values then relate to desired ends, decisions about the proper means to these ends are ethical judgments. These matters are intricately interwoven and do not separate easily for discussion. In one sense members of both divisions share common goals—to live the good life and be well thought of by their fellows. But these seemingly common goals are based on and defined by differing premises, emphasize different standards. I will try to show how these groups differ in their interpretation of the good life and the good person, and what characteristics each uses in judging and evaluating their fellow man. Values, purposes, means, ends may not unravel well, but the basic idea should be clear—prestige accrues to those who best fit the model of the ideal person held by the members of the group that "counts" for the individual. If there are two contrasting social groups on the reservation, the ideals and attendant evaluations should differ accordingly.

Values of the White-Oriented Group

The category "white-oriented" and the characteristics by which it is defined in the context of the study, intimates that this group, in most respects, approximates the social structuring and culture of the American community of which the reservation is a part. The values of this segment of the reservation population are assumed to be similar to those found in a neighboring non-Indian community. The present purpose is not to analyze thoroughly either white-oriented or American values, but to establish that there is a similarity between the two, and to sketch the background against which a contrasting Indian-oriented value pattern stands out. The values can be abstracted from statements occurring repeatedly among the interview data, and they can be compared with some American value orientation about which there is agreement.

The values expressed in the field-interview data that appear to be most useful in separating the white-oriented from the Indian-oriented are closely related to those that were abstracted, in Chapter 4, from the speeches of governmental officials of the 1880s: work, self-dependence, individualism, and acquisitiveness. These are highly interrelated concepts. Work is a means by which to achieve valued ends, in this case independence from others, the accumulation of property for self-security and the security of one's immediate family. It is also an end in itself. It is good to work. A man who is known as a good worker gains some prestige in the community. A white-oriented man uses these values as a measure of others whether or not he appears to practice them himself.

Some of these valued characteristics were indicated in the economic data gathered from my sample (McFee 1962:114–124) and some of those findings are reviewed to show that the values are reflected in actual behavior. Only three of the twenty white-oriented men were irregularly employed. Two were regularly employed at seasonal labor, but all others had year around employment. Again, the relative dependence upon family support and welfare aid appeared to be significant. Twelve of the twenty received no family support, three others did, but they were active participants in a successful family ranch or farm enterprise. Only one white-oriented man reported use of welfare.[14]

These figures, of course, reflect the influence of other factors, such as economic potential, relative age, education, health, and opportunity. But they are related also to motivation and to the degree of commitment to the white-oriented value system. The following excerpts, paraphrased from interviews with white-oriented subjects, illustrate some of the ways these values are expressed.

> I've been ranching all my life, and had to get a fee patent—they held me down. The reservation rules tied you all up. I'm independent and have trained the kids to be the same. I wanted to build up the ranch for the boys. Two of them

---

[14] These and the following figures, based on the answers given by members of the sample to my questionnaire are used to indicate some trends apparent in the limited data. Because of the small and incomplete sample it would not be safe to treat these trends as well supported generalizations about the whole population.

are running it now. The youngest . . . isn't set up. He's working for the railroad, but there's no future in that. You work for them for forty years and all you have is a pension, and then you only work six months a year if you're lucky.
—mixed-blood rancher

I worked with a fellow about my age whose mother always complained. "My poor boy, always having to work." It made me sore. Why shouldn't he? I've always worked. I tried taking some time off work once and about went crazy.
The people [Indians] just don't understand what they're up against. They're looking for someone to take care of them.
—mixed-blood business man

No wonder the Indians are a happy-go-lucky bunch. They don't have to work. Lease money, per capita, and relief keep them going. They need to be put on their own and made to work their way out of it.
After I graduated from high school the old man talked to me and asked me what I was going to do. He said I couldn't just run around in the car, I had to do something. I've always had a job and haven't had to ask the people for anything.
—mixed-blood business employee

My parents emphasized hard work, honesty, thrift, and education. The Indians are clannish, but I'm more of a lone wolf. I'd rather take care of myself than to get help from the family.
I have fee patent title to my land so I can make my own deals without all the red tape and delay that you get at the agency.
The best days were under Stone and Campbell when everybody had a farm and was working.
—full-blood, self-employed contractor

Indians drop out of college because they haven't learned the value of an education. They can't manage their own affairs. In college it's all up to you. I have a tribal scholarship and work during vacations. I have an interest in the family ranch and help there and work for other ranchers too.
—mixed-blood college student

Many more clues appeared scattered through the interview data, and gained additional support from observation. White-oriented people prefer to be busy. They do not spend much time with the street corner groups. In fact a good indicator of orientation may be the time a person spends in such gatherings. Only the more elderly white-oriented men can stand or sit quietly and comfortably in conversation for any length of time. Most seem to have to be actively talking or listening. They jiggle their change or their keys. They look about more often and with quicker head movements than the Indians. In a comparatively short time the white-oriented person moves off down the street or into a building, off about their "business" or giving that impression, at least. The Indian-oriented on the other hand, can stand or sit quietly for an hour, two hours, or most of the day and do not feel compelled to talk all the time if nothing need be said. "Busyness" is not so important for them as it is for the white-oriented.

Often in white-oriented families both husband and wife hold steady jobs, and in some cases both are working and saving to develop a ranch or business for future economic independence. Compared to the Indian-oriented, the white-oriented persons are more concerned about the education and future of their children; they encourage them to go on to college, or to get other training beyond high school. They give more attention to improving their homes, and feel the need to buy and maintain furniture, appliances, equipment, and automobiles. They early encourage their children to take on responsibility for chores, to work and to plan for their future. They cannot understand how anyone could think and act otherwise, unless they are "lazy and immoral."

The values expressed in the interviews and observations are similar, in kind, to those commonly attributed to middle-class Americans. The emphasis upon and appreciation of work, self-dependence, individualism, and acquisitiveness noted in the above quotations, and the additional characteristics of concern for education and for the future, are all recognized, under one name or another, in the social science studies of American values.

In one such study, Williams, a sociologist, recognizes the difficulty of isolating a common set of values for a large, complex, and heterogeneous society (Williams 1970:450), but finds support for fourteen major "value orientations," which are "certain dominant themes [abstracted] from the many important regional, class, and other intracultural variations" (Williams 1970:452–453).

Work is mentioned both as a valued means to other ends, and as an end in itself, and is subsumed as one aspect of the "Activity and Work" orientation. Activity is stressed and, according to Williams, ". . . it is no accident that business so characteristic of the culture can also be spelled 'busy-ness.' " (Williams 1970:458–461). Self-dependence and individualism are included as constituents of an orientation called "Individual Personality": "to be a person is to be independent, responsible, and self respecting, and thereby to be worthy of concern and respect in one's own right" (Williams 1970:495). The emphasis upon acquisitiveness is included in the "Material Comfort" orientation; a condition that "is highly approved and sought after." The material comfort orientation, according to Williams, does not reveal the "specific values . . . involved," which appear to be complexly interwoven in the idea of the "American Standard of Living" with its

undertones and overtones of meanings—from nationalistic identification, to symbols of success, competence, and power and from a token of moral excellence to something very close to a terminal goal at the level of hedonistic gratification (Williams 1970:469–470).

At this level of analysis it would appear safe to assume that the value orientations of the white-oriented sub-culture are broadly similar to the values of the general American public. They are consistent with the economic, social and cultural life of the nation. The individual ideals of success, prestige, and higher status, achievable through the expression of these valued characteristics are considered contributory to the progress of the country. These values are a part of the complex American culture, and are linked with expectations that success will follow upon their practice. The white-oriented Blackfeet have learned these expectations through experience and example.

Values of the Indian-Oriented Group

The characteristics valued by the traditional Blackfeet, mentioned in Chapter 3, still persist in attenuated form. The changing conditions of life have required, however, that new avenues for their expression be found. At first glance such things as bravery, skill, wisdom, and generosity appear to be characteristics that would be valued by the average American. In order to understand how Indian-oriented and white-oriented definitions of these differ, it is necessary to recognize that since the life goals of the two groups are not the same, the premises from which value judgments are made are not the same.

The white-oriented values were seen to be consistent with the national economy and culture, and sufficiently integrated with these to be both vehicles to individual prestige and expressions of national goals. White Americans and white-oriented Blackfeet work toward their own and the nation's security, and to build a better future for their children.

As was shown in Chapter 4, the Indians had little choice but to accept the economic system of the dominant society and were pressed to accept the white values that went with it. To date the Indian-oriented, in general, have experienced little economic success and, perhaps because of this, have not adopted the values. In turn, the persistence of traditional values has contributed, in part, to this lack of economic success. This will be examined later. It is assumed that the present values of the Indian-oriented are the result of both persistence of traditional traits and new interpretations of these developed during the attempts at economic readaptation.

Because the Indian-oriented have developed no expectancy of success in the white man's economy, they have become neither imbued with the associated values nor committed fully to white goals. Instead they appear to have made more explicit what was once an implicit life goal of Indian society—to retain their ethnic identity. I make this inference from statements about "keeping the old ways alive," "showing the young people the things from the past," and from the attachment people show to bundles, regalia, doing Indian craft and art work, and other "Indian" symbols. The major common goal, hence a prime value, of the Indian-oriented society is to be *Indian*, and the present value judgments can be understood best as they relate to this goal. To illustrate this relationship, values are isolated that in reality are intricately interdependent.

Individualism, a valued characteristic in the old culture, is highly valued today. The Indian is concerned with individual achievement, social acceptance, increased prestige, and higher status, interests he shares with the white-oriented, but the expression of these values by individuals of the two orientations differs in light of their separate goals.

The differences show up clearly in the way that Indian-oriented parents tend to treat their children. Ideally, children are seen as little individuals whose rights and wishes should be respected. They should be guided and directed, but not forced into doing things. Indian parents think that white people are being cruel when they spank their children; teasing and ridicule are acceptable correctives. Children are wanted, loved but not coddled; no elaborate concern is expressed when they get bumps. Injuries are cared for, assurances given, and then everybody's attention turns to other things.

Babies and young children go wherever their parents go, with little concern shown about feeding and sleeping schedules. Children are at most public gatherings and play about quite freely regardless of the occasion. At one political rally I was sitting behind a young couple who were letting their son play with his father's keys. The rattling of the keys often made it hard to hear what was said, but nobody objected. Several times the keys fell to the floor with a loud clatter. I thought, hopefully, that that would end the game, but each time the father picked up the keys and gave them back to his son. I interpreted this to mean that the child's interests were as important as anyone else's.

A mother might suggest several times that her child share a toy with another, but the matter is dropped if the child is persistent in refusing. Children make many such decisions for themselves, because it is their right to do so. If they get too far out of line they will be ridiculed. This attitude continues throughout their lives. A school official told me about his frustration when a bright young student decided, against his urging, not to go to college. The boy's father was easily convinced and offered to push the case with his son, but returned several days later to report that he had tried. His son had said no, he did not want to go. That ended the matter. White-oriented men reported that their fathers rarely took no for an answer.

Present-day Indian-oriented people still have the strong emotional commitment to their name and self-image that was an attribute of the Blackfeet in the horse and buffalo days. Indian and white informants alike mention jealousy as a strong Indian personality trait and blame this for the inability of the Indian-oriented group to unite in support of any specific program. This self-concern perpetuates shame and gossip as powerful agents of social control. Other contrasting interpretations of individualism become apparent in later descriptions of the requisites for status within the Indian-oriented group.

Bravery, once manifest in war, hunting, and horse raiding, remains a valued characteristic. Ewers noted this in Blackfeet patriotism and their response to World Wars I and II. Many young men enlisted, the relatives of many honored them at a feast, and old men sang war songs and prayed for their success (Ewers 1955:322; 1958:324). Blackfeet continue to serve in our overseas conflicts. But in modern life the opportunities for achieving distinction by the regular exhibition of bravery are limited. This quality contributes to success in occasional fights, sports, and rodeos, and in some kinds of employment—the ranch hand and the fire fighter often have their bravery tested. But it is no longer a chief requisite for economic and social achievement. Other attributes are given greater recognition.

Skill is important today. Because Indian identification is the goal, abilities that contribute to this end are valued by the Indian-oriented; dancing, singing, art, crafts, and oratorical skills are recognized as important to the expression of ethnic identity. Several women are well known for their leather and beading work; the Blackfeet Art Association furthers the work of many tutored and untutored wood carvers and painters.

It was suggested that Indians participate in sports and rodeos because these were related to traditional Indian activities, and because Indian success in these activities had been given recognition by white people. Skills in these events are highly regarded by the Indian-oriented, perhaps for these same reasons.

The people of this group gain subsistence within the white economic system so that work skills become important. For the most part the Indians must work to get money to buy the necessities of life and the other things they want. Work is the principal means by which to acquire goods and property, and competence at work increases the chances both of finding work and making more money. In addition, work skills are valued as indices of personal achievement. Indian acquaintances identify themselves and others with some comment about what a man is, does, or has done, and past or present economic abilities are included in this appraisal. Unemployed men, talking to a white observer, usually point out past accomplishments, jobs at which they excel, or catalog the land, stock, and other possessions they own that might impress the investigator with their personal worth. Remember that John Arrowhead recalled that he had been a "champion dancer" and "a good bronc rider." He had traveled and worked in many parts of the country, he said, and told many stories of his adventures during those times. He took me on a tour of his "land" to show the house, ranch, and stock he owned. The land was his undoubtedly, but all else belonged to the leaseholder.

This suggests another reason why economic skills, like excellence at sports, are valued by the Indian-oriented. They are aware that these skills and abilities are given recognition by their white and white-oriented neighbors. Not only do these accomplishments contribute toward earning a living and a sense of personal achievement, but they also enhance the image of "the Indian" among the white men.

The Indian-oriented value work skills but have not adopted the American appreciation of work as an end in itself. Some of this is reflected in the responses to my questionnaire. None of the eight men from the sample who were classified as Indian-oriented were regularly employed. Four of these owned land and earned some lease income from that; five received some financial support from other family members, while three had been dependent on welfare to get them through the year. Neither these nor the figures given above for the white-oriented are exactly representative of their respective groups, that is, not all white-oriented people are well off, nor are all Indian-oriented poor, but a comparison of these indicators does show the generally lower economic position of the Indian-oriented. The Indian works hard and well but feels no compulsion to work beyond the time necessary to satisfy short-term needs. Several factors contribute to this attitude, such as the irregular and seasonal jobs the Indian-oriented people are accustomed to getting, the apparent lack of interest in many things the white man considers essential, and the social restrictions on accumulation of property which will be discussed under the heading of generosity. Local, state and bureau school officials met to discuss problems of Indian education during one of my visits. Several speakers claimed that the Indian children were low on motivation and high on the scale of dropouts. One official recognized the value discrepancy when he stated,

"You won't achieve your educational goals until you teach the Indians to want what you want." The Indian-oriented value social participation, visiting, attending Pow Wows on this and other reservations, horse races, and stick games more than long and steady labor. You do not have to work endlessly if you prefer social participation to extra furniture, appliances, a lawn, and a savings account. It is difficult for persons with this attitude to win acceptance and high status within the white-oriented structure.

Wisdom, too, is valued to the degree that it contributes to the maintenance of Indian-ness. Thus knowledge of the old religion, lore, and rituals is highly regarded, even by the Indian-oriented who no longer believe in them. One inform-ant commented, "I know I'm full-blooded and like to keep the old things alive." A woman was disappointed to hear that there would be no Sun Dance at the 1960 Indian Days Encampment:

> Indian Days aren't any good if they don't hold the Medicine Lodge. The dances don't have any meaning unless they have the Lodge. I'd take part if they had one. Even if you don't believe in it it's part of old Indian ways. You make prom-ises to people. You have to help them, so you give things and help.

Modern knowledge is also good. But the Indian-oriented, in general, display an ambivalence in their attitudes toward education and it is difficult to isolate the many factors that inhibit Blackfeet progress in school. Among these would be, the gap between home and school environments and the language problem. Chil-dren raised in homes where English is a second language do not have the rein-forcing context of constant use to increase their language ability. Books and magazines, too, would not be available to be used to further develop language and reading skills. The effects of failure and fear of failure in relation to the Indians concern with self-image are also undoubtedly important. Motivation is limited by these and is not overridden by parental authority. The Indian-oriented may urge their children to attend school but, like the men the school official told about, do not order them to do so. As individuals, children have the right to make their own decisions—after they get beyond the age where the truant officer makes it for them.

The Indian-oriented leaders value the knowledge that comes from school and in general support the idea of education. The knowledge gained is valuable and necessary if the Indians are to deal successfully with the white man. Indians can combat white ways by learning from them,[15] but this goal is hard to translate into meaningful immediate objectives for the children. They accept the idea of schooling but find the subjects they study uninteresting and unrelated to any personal goals they might formulate. Many of the jobs available on the reserva-tion do not require much schooling, so many Indian families do not provide an example of the economic returns that counsellors say follow a good education. A well-educated Indian-oriented leader expressed his thoughts on this problem as it related to college attendance:

---

[15] A form of antagonistic acculturation. See Devereaux and Loeb 1943:133–147.

Many of our smart children have disappointed us. They didn't go ahead as they planned. Money problems was one reason, but many had no vital interest. They really didn't know what they wanted to take when they went to school. Because of this they found the courses uninteresting and discouraging.

Wisdom and knowledge, of both old and new ways, serve other ends but appear to be most highly valued when they contribute to the major goal of being Indian. Both Indian- and white-oriented people value wisdom, but the contrasting goals lead to the accenting of different realms of knowledge and the uses to which it is put.

Generosity is a key value of Indian-oriented persons that has survived with the least amount of reinterpretation. It is considered an important requisite to being an Indian and, as such, appears to provide the major motivation for acquiring skill and wisdom. People are expected to share with others and to help those less forutnate than themselves.

Generosity takes both private and public forms. Indian-oriented persons are hospitable and feel a responsibility to care for others that insures that the improvident, aged, disabled or sick will be provided with the minimum requirements of existence. This relatively private form of generosity is relieved somewhat by welfare and charitable sources, but often these are not enough and some people need the help of family and neighbors to make it through the winter. In some cases those on welfare may be considered to be better off than others, and their grown children turn to them for help that is seldom refused.

Public generosity covers the various "give-away" ceremonies mentioned in earlier chapters. This giving is largely a reciprocal gift exchange among peers. No strict accounting is kept of gifts and repayments, but the reciprocity is recognized and people joke about giving blankets to a visiting friend so they can get them back next year when they visit the other reservation. Private generosity by all and public display by a few are forms of generosity that are expected and are controlled ultimately by expressions of public opinion. Many people act generously and spontaneously because it is the right thing to do; others give more begrudgingly because of fear of social disapproval. A person who fails to provide what is expected is called "stingy," and undisputed stinginess causes a person to lose standing within the Indian-oriented group. People do not take chances that might start such talk. Thus the discussion completes the circle back to self-concern and the controlled expression of individualism. A white official told of an incident that sounded probable even though its authenticity could not be checked.

A woman asked him to order a young man out of her house. He had moved in with the family and was just hanging around, eating their food, and making no effort to help out. When the official suggested that she was the one to tell him to leave, she replied that she could not do that. But it would be all right if he would come and do it for her: "Only don't tell that I said for you to do it." Another man had returned to take up residence on the reservation after being away for several years. But the pressures for generosity and the compulsion to follow the rules made him think he had better leave again. "This town breaks you; too many friends that want money and rides here and there."

Candidates for council offices often make gifts of a dollar or two to prospective voters as evidence of their generosity, an act that is criticized if the man has not been helpful in the past. "At election time they're always willing to lend you a dollar, but after they're in they won't give you a nickel." Past generosity, however, can pay off. "They told me not to vote for him, that he wouldn't do a good job. I think that's right, but I voted for him anyway because he always helps people that need it." The feasting at Indian Days, bundle openings, song services, and the political rallies appears to be another form of generosity display.

Generosity can block successful economic adaptation. Ewers wrote that sharing and generosity survived in the 1940s and that the "drain of the 'have-nots' upon the 'haves' has the effect of limiting the economic progress of ambitious individuals" and possibly was "inhibiting the desire of fullbloods of extensive family connections to achieve material success" (Ewers 1955:321–322). In 1959 and 1960 three cases were known, and others reported, where land was sold for large sums of money. Relatives and friends moved in with the recipients and spent several days celebrating the sale. Some stayed to live with the now 'rich' friend or relative. This is reported to be a common practice that has caused the rapid depletion of such income and returned numerous, now landless, Indians to poverty and the welfare rolls.

Often this is more than economic reciprocity. It is a necessary adaptive arrangement for the poor. The economic flow may be one way with the returns, if any, very difficult to assess. In 1959 I visited the home of an elderly woman who had received a large oil bonus payment several years earlier. The money was held in trust by the B.I.A. and she was given regular payments from this account to cover her living expenses. She lived in a good house in town and had living with her at the time two adult sons and several grandchildren. Several other people seemed to come and go, including an elderly couple—a son-in-law by a previous marriage and his present wife. This wife told me that she came by occasionally to help with the housework, and that every week the old lady received her money from the superintendent. "She gives me $5.00, my husband $5.00 and $15.00 to her eldest son." It appeared that quite a few people were partially dependent upon her largess. When the old woman died it was discovered that her account was depleted and she was in debt. The household broke up, the people scattered to fend for themselves, and the now vacant house is falling apart. The reciprocity seemed to be mainly in chores and social support provided by a circle of dependent kin and friends.

The emphasis on generosity has still another face. Too much success, too much accumulation of unshared property, brings the quick reaction of gossip. "He's stingy." "He's trying to live like a white man." "They get all the cattle and won't let us have any." Only a very few who wish to be accepted by the Indian-oriented have been able to walk the fine line between stinginess and generosity. These few have become economically self-sufficient and yet retained a name for generosity among their following by judicious and controlled giving.

Summary

The Indian- and white-oriented groups share some values that appear to be congruent but are seen to have differing definitions. Members of both groups, for instance, would acknowledge that it is good to be generous, but the white-oriented man qualifies his generosity by a prior emphasis upon self-support. It is not good to carry generosity to a fault by impoverishing one's self and family as Indian-oriented men are wont to do. The Indian values work and acquisition of property as a means to an end, but does not agree with the white-oriented persons who see these qualities as ends in themselves.

The values are defined differently according to the different assumptions about the good man and the good life of the two groups. White-oriented activities are directed toward future progress, an end the Indian-oriented find unrealistic. Past experiences have provided no basis for optimism about the future. The major goal of the latter group appears to be the maintenance of Indian identity, and the value judgments are influenced by this end.

The feeling of circularity that wells up in this and other discussions of values, goals, means, ends, purposes, and so on, reflects, I believe, the very circularity of the social scene. People learn to value the things valued by their group, to behave in ways that are acceptable to the group to which they do or aspire to belong. Self-concern may be both the motive for general conformity as well as the root of control; self-concern and concern for status make one responsive to gossip and criticism as well as contributing to one's being a follower and supporter of valued ideals and practices. Membership in one group requires approximation of standards that differ from and may militate against membership in the other. Adding this dimension to the contrasting patterns of association further supports the view that these are separate societies. The value patterns of each group are used by the group members as bases from which to judge the social worth of their neighbors, and the values are reflected in the assignment of the status positions that are considered next.

8

Status

Introduction

THE NATURE AND SEPARATENESS of the two orientation systems are illustrated in this chapter by a review of the status patterns within each group. People conform to a particular set of norms and adopt the related values of the group with which they wish to identify, and acquire a higher or lower status within the group according to how well they exhibit valued characteristics. The status systems of the two orientation groups are examined here to identify areas of contrast and to suggest the nature of intragroup leadership and social organization.

Economic achievement plays a more important role in defining status among the white-oriented people that it does among the Indian-oriented, and a man's house is one important symbol of how well he is doing economically. I use housing, therefore, in my discussion of status among the white-oriented group, but do not give similar treatment to Indian-oriented housing because they do not give this much weight in judging their peers. In the proper place I will describe some Indian-oriented homes and then take the opportunity to point out some characteristics of home furnishing and maintenance that seem to follow from the differing values of the two groups. The general economic and housing conditions on the reservation must be remembered, however, to avoid making hasty inferences.

The visitor to the reservation sees much substandard housing which he is apt to register in his head as "Indian housing." He is right in one sense; most of the houses are occupied by tribal members, but he is in error if he thinks that this is the kind of housing the Blackfeet prefer. The descriptions in Chapter 4 should have made it clear that poverty and poor housing are both prevalent, and while these two tend to go hand in hand, home construction on the reservation has been hindered greatly because trust lands could not be mortgaged, as well as for lack of money. The present housing programs have taken a decade or more of planning, land purchase, condemnations, and financial maneuvering to get under way and are just beginning to allow the abandonment of some hundreds of shanties, shacks, and cabins that have accumulated over the past half-century.

My analysis of the economic data gathered from my sample clearly demonstrated widespread poverty, but not everybody is poor—there are relatively affluent people both among the Indian- and white-oriented groups. The differences within each group are probably greater than those between them, but the average standing of Indian-oriented people, as a whole, is lower than that of the white-oriented (McFee 1962:120–124). To the extent that there is a positive correlation between income and housing, then, it is to be expected that a higher percentage of the Indian-oriented live in substandard housing than do the white-oriented. In what follows, then, I assume that adequate housing is desired by all and difficult to come by regardless of cultural orientation: the maintenance and furnishing of whatever kind of house people live in, however, does seem to me to be a fair indicator of some of the value differences described in the preceding chapter. This is what I will be talking about when I mention housing.

It should also be remembered that my sample was male so that much of what follows may reflect a male emphasis. Women play an integral part in establishing the status of the family. They maintain the homes, raise the children, and often contribute to the family income as well. All in all their influence often may be more important than that of the men in status achievement. A study of women and their role in reservation life is sorely needed.

Status among the White-Oriented

The white-oriented society can be divided roughly into three status classes: low, middle, and high. Class boundaries are indistinct, but high status can be distinguished from low, while the middle class shades imperceptibly into the two extremes forming what Stern, in his Klamath study so aptly called a "status gradient" (Stern 1966:214ff).

WHITE-ORIENTED LOW STATUS Low status people generally, are the least educated and least trained in the skills essential to regular employment. Consequently they are often irregularly employed, live in poor houses, dress poorly, and have few possessions. Poverty is a condition shared by low status people of both groups.

White and white-oriented people tend to lump low status people together regardless of orientation. While this is reasonable by many criteria, such judgments overlook cultural factors that make a white-oriented man different than his Indian-oriented counterpart. These distinguishing characteristics will be seen more clearly in the later discussion of the low status Indian-oriented.

The low status stratum encompasses a range from hard working, but irregularly employed men at the top, to a few improvident individuals at the bottom of the scale. The more ambitious of this class actively seek work and are considered to be good workers by those who know them. However, the jobs they find are seasonal and provide insufficient income for economic stability.

In general, low status men express little commitment to success and prog-

Sub-standard housing. Note the evidence of attention to interior housekeeping and the definition of a yard.

ress. One of the men interviewed had gone to Denver under a federal relocation program, but found the work too difficult so returned to his family. Another remarked that the relocation program was intended to help the Indian find work. He, with an average annual income of $2,250, had thought about going on relocation, but never applied. "I don't have much trouble getting a job," he said.

None of the low status men I interviewed own their own homes. Two talked about fixing things up around the houses they occupied but have not made improvements that would be expected if they were concerned about material comfort. Housing appears to be poor and inadequate when eight to eleven people live in a two room shack. In 1960 I visited a man who had lived with his wife and eight children in a house owned by one of his relatives. This was an old, two-room, unpainted structure with shiplap outer walls that had been patched here and there with plyboard. Some of the original asphalt roof remained visible among the many patches that had been applied over the years. The ceiling and some of the interior walls were covered with wallboard, others with cardboard. A single light bulb suspended from the ceiling by its cord hung in each room. Well worn linoleum covered the floors. The rooms were simply furnished: a wooden table, wooden chairs, an old overstuffed chair, a kitchen storage cabinet, two fiberboard wardrobes, a chest of drawers, three double beds, and a crib. A wall-hung kitchen sink with a cold water tap was the extent of interior plumbing; a wood range served for both cooking and heating. Family photographs, two Charles Russell prints, dishes, family keepsakes, a radio, a throw rug, and a few other possessions were on display. The interior of the house was crowded, but neat, orderly, and well-scrubbed; the exterior was stained, cracked, and in disrepair. A sagging fence partially marked off a yard area between the house and an outdoor toilet. Two shrubs grew as evidence of an early attempt to garden and there was considerable debris scattered about the dirt and weeds that made up the yard. To me there appeared to be much that needed to be done to make the place livable, yet when I asked this man, seasonally employed with an income of about $2,500, about the availability of federal or tribal home improvement loans, I was told: "Yes they have a setup for that. I guess we could get a loan like that if we needed it." I do not know if this family still lives in this house, but it is there today. The only visible changes through the years have been further deterioration and the addition of a television antenna.

When asked about future plans, these men have little to offer. They express little expectation beyond returning to the old job, or finding a similar one, each spring. The inference is that they are not dissatisfied with present conditions. Family responsibilities, lack of credit, uncertain employment, the weather and the seasons are the factors that govern the economic condition of the low status men. It is unlikely that these men can be "successful" but they try; the idlers are those who have given up.

The improvident ones, at the bottom of the scale have lost any initiative they once might have had. Most of these, like their Indian-oriented counterparts, are called "winos" and "bums" by their fellow townsmen. Some are alcoholics in fact, others in name only. These men are community problem cases—the concern of the police and welfare authorities.

Yet these men are white-oriented in spite of the apparent lack of commitment to the values of their group. First of all, they are not Indian-oriented. They know little or nothing of Indian language or customs and do not take part in Indian social activities, nor do they seek Indian identity. Secondly, the low status white-oriented persons have the knowledge and habits of their group. They are peripheral participants in the economic, political, and social life of their community. Those who work are rewarded with the accolade, "a good worker," which puts them on a rung above the improvident on the status ladder. But they have little influence or social standing. Low status people do not run for political offices; they are neither members of service clubs or other organizations, nor do they take part in the P.T.A., Youth Club, Boy or Girl Scout, or 4-H Club work. Low status persons spend their spare time with members of their families or with others of similar status. Reported recreational activities include hunting and fishing, card games with neighbors or family, an occasional movie, driving around in a car with friends, and drinking.

Low income, irregular labor, and limited participation are the interrelated characteristics that most clearly separate the low from the middle status. Lack of training contributes to a low income; poverty, in turn, limits both self-improvement and social participation.

WHITE-ORIENTED MIDDLE STATUS The middle status white-oriented class includes the majority of the white-oriented group and, in reality, is more a convenient collection of a series of gradually changing ranks than it is a single status position. The people who occupy these status positions, however, share a few general characteristics: they are (1) regularly employed, (2) committed to individual progress, (3) active participants in community affairs, and (4) they clearly support and exemplify the white-oriented values.

Individuals in this classification represent a wide range of economic and social achievement. Occupations of middle status people range from regularly employed craftsmen through clerical workers in business, agency, and council to businessmen, politicians, small farmers, and ranchers. Not all are financially independent, but all are building toward that goal. This is a characteristic that stands out in the interview materials. These people think about their future and the future of their children—they have plans for tomorrow. It shows in "Bob Sorrel Horse's dream" reported by a poor white-oriented full-blood rancher, who, by his industry may just qualify for middle status even though his annual cash income seldom exceeds $2,000:

> I have this dream to get some money and fix this place up right—a nice house and a good place. First, I'd get electricity in to pump the water. I had planned to remodel the house . . . to have a place I'm not ashamed of.

Yet while he dreams, this man acts. He cared for his small herd of thirteen head of cattle and a few horses, had a sound shelter and well-maintained corrals for the stock. The grounds around the house were uncluttered, all garbage and debris was in one pile some distance from the house. A good supply of firewood was cut and stacked near the house. A clothesline, outhouse, and small utility shed were all in good order.

The house in which six people lived was an old log structure with two rooms on the ground floor and one loft room above. It was well chinked and the old hand split shake roof was in good repair. Water was carried from a pitcher pump mounted at the well a few feet from the cabin door; there was no electricity, and gas lanterns provided the light. A wood range provided the heat. The interior walls were painted, cotton curtains hung at the windows and a worn rug covered part of the linoleum floor. The home furnishings consisted of a painted washstand, wooden table, wooden chairs, a kitchen cupboard, one double and two single beds, homemade closets, a nightstand, and a high chair. Family photos, a calendar, a radio, two rifles, fishing gear, and other family possessions were to be seen. The children's bicycle, tricycles, wagon, and a stroller were stored in the shed out back. A zinc washtub hanging outside on the front wall of the cabin provided the clue to the laundry facilities. Everything was worn, clean, orderly and in good repair. This man was poor, yet he maintained what he had and dreamed of something better in the future.

At the upper end of the scale, this same concern for the future is expressed by the well-to-do rancher, quoted in the earlier chapter, who built up his ranch for the boys and was concerned that the youngest son had no future with the railroad.

Middle status people join the service clubs, farm and cattle associations, and support and participate in community improvement projects. The leaders of F.F.A., 4-H, Boy and Girl Scouts, and the Youth Club are either whites or tribal members of this class. These people sponsor the Easter Egg Hunts, the Fishing Derbies, local sports events, and often the rodeos. They are not always the leaders, but are the active supporters of community, church, and school enterprises.

Middle status people are active politically. Tribal council positions and a few county elective offices are sought and often won by people of this classification, and they are actively supported or opposed, advised or criticized, by their peers.

People of middle status tend to live in well-constructed, well-maintained

Two kinds of rural housing.

homes. For example, Ray Hawkins, whose annual income was about $3,500, lived with his wife and four children in a four room frame house. It was freshly painted inside and out and the composition roof was in good condition at the time of my visit. There was a fenced yard, with lawn and flower beds, an outdoor fireplace and a picnic table. This house had electricity, inside plumbing with both hot and cold water supplied to the bathroom and kitchen. The interior walls were all lined and painted; the floors were wooden, covered with cotton rugs in the living room and bedrooms and with linoleum in the kitchen and bath. The comparatively large kitchen had built-in cabinets around and over the sink, an electric range and refrigerator, a heavy dining table, and solid wood chairs. There were cotton curtains at the windows. The bedrooms had built-in closets, beds and chests of drawers. The living room was well furnished with a fairly new davenport and living room chairs, each with its antimacassar. There was a coffee table, an ottoman, a piano, table lamps, a record player, and a radio. The windows were draped and family photographs, some of the children's art work, music, and numerous books were on display.

Not all middle status persons have good homes, but evidence of improvement is apparent in the houses they do have. This may amount to anything from a fresh coat of paint on interior walls to a new roof, a new entryway, or the addition of one or more rooms. When I reviewed the data from my sample, I noted that two of the fourteen homes of white-oriented middle status sample members were scored excellent and nine good. The middle status people do not all plant lawns and gardens, but with rare exceptions, all lawns and gardens on the reservation are planted by middle or high status white or white-oriented people.

Home improvement, and a tendency toward the acquisition of more appliances and other possessions with increased income, demonstrate the underlying values of acquisitiveness and material comfort. White-oriented people, above the low status category, buy, use, and care for more home furnishings and appliances. A middle-class American would recognize an air of material comfort that goes beyond utility, memorabilia, and decoration, and differs in this respect from the average Indian-oriented home regardless of financial condition. This elusive and hard to define impression may become clearer by contrast with Indian-oriented homes described later.

The white-oriented tend to identify home and possessions with family status. One white community leader, acquainted with sociological literature, assessed the class positions of the town, and used home improvement as a key to attempted upward mobility. Even Indian-oriented people are aware of this "have things" aspect of white living. An Indian who acquires too many appliances and other home furnishings is accused of "trying to live like a white man."

WHITE-ORIENTED HIGH STATUS   Highest status among the white-oriented persons is held by a few men or families who own large farms or ranches, or operate successful businesses. In most respects they resemble the middle status people in that they are industrious, ambitious, acquisitive, and active in community affairs. These people, however, stand out for their greater success. They are financially independent, have larger, well-maintained, and better furnished homes like that of Henry Rogers described in Chapter 1. They are leaders in community enterprises and politics and, further, they meet on more equal terms with the white business leaders of the community and region.

In addition to the economic and social attributes just mentioned, these men share a broad knowledge of men and events beyond the local scene. Their interests lead them into contact with men of like interests beyond the reservation and county boundaries. They have traveled widely and have a lively interest in American history, politics, and business affairs.

The economic independence attained by these men has left them freer to pursue other affairs. They can afford to spend more time in public service work. All have become interested in improving the conditions of the reservation population. I mentioned earlier the two who had learned about Blackfeet culture in later life, and display a great interest in the Indians. They know this culture intellectually but have not internalized an Indian point of view. These people have white values and goals and, whether they realize it or not, are working to change the Indians toward a greater acceptance of white ways. Like the government officials, they feel that the opportunity for steady work and a good education will solve most of the problems faced by the Indian. Remember, too, Henry Rogers' idea that the council should buy some grass and flower seed to give to all the householders in town. He and other high status people are pleased that the low rent and mutual aid housing programs include lawns in the plans. His suggestion and these plans are realistic from the point of view of those who subscribe to white-oriented values, but overlook the fact that the Indians do not share these same values. It will be interesting to watch the results of the planting programs to see whether or not the Indian-oriented occupants care to maintain these lawns.

The man I called Harry Wilson has a different view of the Indian because of what he learned about Blackfeet culture as a child during the few years he spent with his Indian stepgrandfather on a Canadian reserve. Before and after this visit, he was raised in a completely white-oriented home, but as a consequence of this training and the considerable participation in Indian society that it allowed, he has a deeper understanding of the Indian-oriented people. His idea of service is to help them maintain their own culture. He is able to take part in their ritual and social activities, but serves primarily at a managerial level with the local and national committees that promote pan-Indian celebrations, arts and crafts. This man is white-oriented, but has had experience that enables him to empathize with the Indian. He helps the Indian-oriented to affirm their traditions, while others of his class can only affirm their own and try to help the Indians by changing them.

Perhaps because of their greater association with white people, the high status white-oriented, and a few in the class below who approach this status, are the ones most conscious of social discrimination or at least most vocal about it. I asked everybody I interviewed about this and people at this social level had the strongest feelings about it. The complaints were less about discrimination in the economic sphere than about social slights. One man stated that everyone gets on well until some white businessman's daughter becomes too interested in a mixed-blood boy. The white parents soon step in and break it up. A woman complained that she was never invited to local women's meetings, teas, or other parties, and a study of membership and attendance lists for social groups sponsored by the white business people and agency employees appears to support her contention. The high status white-oriented person is economically and culturally the same as many of his white neighbors. He aspires, and is qualified, to be fully accepted. Away from home he meets little discrimination but, like the man mentioned earlier who became the liquor store manager, his Indian heritage is often held against him in the local and neighboring towns. This discrimination, felt strongly by the persons most nearly integrated into the American society, emphasizes again that the major difference between the white-oriented segment of the tribe and other American people around them is due to their being legally defined Indians, members of an Indian tribe, who live on a reservation. Their white neighbors too easily stereotype all Indians and discriminate against them accordingly without understanding any of them or noting individual differences among them.

It must be noted that the Blackfeet too are caught up in the racist beliefs that are so prevalent in our society. In general, they dislike blacks, foreigners, and, of course, whites. Some Indians expressed dismay when they found that fair housing laws meant that whites could not be excluded from the tribally sponsored but federally funded low rent housing. This observation is made as a part of the description and is in no way intended to excuse discrimination against the Indians.

The status levels of the white-oriented community reflect the scale by which white or white-oriented people assess themselves and their neighbors, and these are congruent with the status patterns of the region, as I explained in a footnote to my earlier report (McFee 1962:178). The white-oriented people are socially, politically, economically and culturally, a part of the mainstream of American life.

As the white-oriented share status and value systems with the white people, they tend to assess the Indians by these same standards. The white-oriented person will tend to place an Indian-oriented person in a class just below his own even when they are equal in most other respects. The improvident Indian is ranked lower than the improvident white. White-oriented people measure all others by their own standards, in relation to themselves and their kind.

The Indian-oriented person, however, sees the relative status of the tribal members from quite a different perspective. Social worth is measured by different standards in Indian-oriented society, and the standards reflect commitment to other values.

Status among the Indian-Oriented

The people of one segment of the Blackfeet Tribe consider themselves the real Blackfeet Indians and dedicate themselves to being Indian. Toward this end they share elements of culture that differ from that of the surrounding population and associate most frequently with people of like orientation. The group has its own measures of status based upon expressions of the values supported by its members, and because of differing goals and values, the status system of the Indian-oriented is incongruent with that of the white-oriented society. The Indian judges his group and the whole tribal population by another standard that results in a dissimilar ranking.

For present purposes the same threefold classification of status—low, middle, and high—is used, but the positions are discussed in another order. In Indian-oriented society, high status is achieved by the attainment of prestige and influence through behaviors that express the values of the group. This is the same general principle that operates among the white-oriented society, but the bicultural situation, in which the Indian-oriented are an economically and politically dependent minority, has opened two avenues to higher status for Indian-oriented people. Low status people are relatively homogeneous, middle status less so, and the high status category can be split into the two types based upon knowledge of and proficiency in the white man's world. Because of this the high status classes are described first, then the low status, followed by a brief description of the large middle class that, by its judgments and support, make or breaks people's status claims. The discussion of the characteristics that make for the achievement of high status will describe best the ideals of the society against which the lower rankings are also measured.

INDIAN-ORIENTED HIGH STATUS   The joint requirements of maintaining Indian identity and achieving this within the political and economic framework of white culture have opened two channels to prestige and leadership within the Indian-oriented group. The ideal leader in this situation would be a man wise in the ways of both traditional Blackfeet and modern American cultures. He would be an authority on how best to be an Indian, yet well educated, skilled, and able to meet the white man on common ground. He would be experienced sufficiently to gain acceptance and influence in white society and to act as an able interpreter of each group to the other. The history of Blackfeet and American relations is too short to have produced such an ideal in one man. Instead, as more and more tribal members become white-oriented, some men gain high status by their greater knowledge of Blackfeet culture as it is known today. These leaders form a least acculturated high status stratum that for the sake of simplicity, will be called the *chiefs*. Others, better educated and more experienced with white culture, find high status by playing the roles of intercultural interpreters and mediators. They are accomplished spokesmen for the Indian-oriented point of view, and as a more acculturated high status class are labeled *interpreters*. There are more than generational differences between these two status types.

Chiefs are usually older men who know and support the currently known traditions and beliefs. They vary in their knowledge, belief and dedication, but all, together, form a repository of what is remembered of the old ways. One of these men recognized that much of the old culture had been lost, "things beyond the memory of even the old timers," but he and others of his status are "trying to show the young people the things from the past," with special emphasis on keeping the language alive. Their qualities and characteristics are those given in the description of Albert Buffalo Heart, so will be only summarily reviewed here.

Through their age, knowledge, and practice of Blackfeet ideals each of these men has gained the respect of a numerous following of kinsmen, friends and people from a particular region who recognize him as their chief, or respected elder. So these men are given respect and loyalty but little political power. It appears that the old leadership structure persists among the Indian-oriented group. People tend to shift their loyalties according to kinship, friendship, and self-interest. The leadership that develops carries responsibilities and influence, but rarely true authority. The chiefs are recognized as links to the past, authorities on tradition, and symbols of the Indian, but as the roles given them will show, these things are peripheral to the present political and economic sphere.

Chiefs perform a variety of public duties that center around their position as authorities on tradition. They serve on the Indian Days committee; they help in planning the program and in the regulation of the camp; they don ceremonial regalia to take part in the dancing and exhibitions that make up the program. If a Sun Dance is held, it should be sponsored by people of this class and the principal roles will be filled by chiefs and their families. They are called upon to greet distinguished visitors and to officiate in adoption ceremonies and giveaways.

Several of these men own medicine bundles that they open on the proper occasions, and they help conduct the ceremonies at the bundle openings of other people. A few know curing practices and rituals and conduct curing ceremonies even though they and their patients also go to white doctors.

Some of the chiefs serve on the Honorary Tribal Council and receive a small per diem for attendance at council meetings. Members of this honorary council are chosen frequently to accompany delegations to the state and national capitals to lobby for or against proposed legislation that might affect the tribe. Both in the council and on such trips, the chiefs see themselves as spokesmen for the full-bloods and take every occasion to speak out, usually in Blackfeet, urging harmony and trust, and requesting more help for "the People"—the full-bloods.

The people, in general, take pride in their old timers but want them to exercise their influence outside of the council. They are handicapped, too, as political leaders because they speak little English and so fail to communicate directly with many of the people they seek to influence. They wish to arrive at decisions by the traditional council method that requires lengthy discussion and unanimity. The dominant culture and society within which they must act, the white and white-oriented leaders that must be influenced, do not allow time for this method of resolving issues. The men are extended the courtesy of free speech, but this does not include giving much attention to what they say.

These men have attained this status by the routes of wisdom, skill, and generosity. Wisdom and skill have developed through their experience. Their fathers, as youths, saw the last of the buffalo days and told their sons about that life, so their tie with the past is real. The chiefs have lived through ¾ of a century of the changes described in Chapter 4, so the wisdom they profess has a basis in experience with the white man. They were active participants in the trials of change, having tried many of the programs for economic readaptation with varying degrees of success. In the course of these economic ups and downs these men accepted some change, but also tried to maintain the traditions as they knew them, a difficult and dangerous job in face of the strenuous efforts of the government to stamp out these traditions. Their ability to do this has made them both the advisers and symbols they now are for numbers of people.

The high status position of these men is fairly stable but still depends on the numbers and support of their followers. Their claims to status must be validated by continued service and acts of generosity. They are not wealthy, but they have shared what they had in better times and perform services presently that validate their positions.

The chiefs do not present a united front, and are still rivals for additional prestige. They criticize one another and are gossiped about by other people. One old man will dismiss the tales of another as "lies." Another will be criticized for telling war stories. "He once put a story in the paper about how he scalped a Crow [Indian]. People laugh at him. He shouldn't tell those stories, they don't belong to him. My daddy told me not to tell these war stories, they're the property of the people who did the things."

The chiefs, then, are honored for their ability to symbolize tradition and to advise about and maintain these traditions. The knowledge and experience that has gained them this status, however, cannot be translated into effective, practical political and economic leadership, so that another type of Indian-oriented leader must fill this gap.

Interpreters,[16] like Raymond Black Plume, form a high status class made up of relatively younger men who are better educated, were raised in Indian-oriented homes, speak both languages fluently, and have assumed, or gained, leadership roles in the community. They express the ambition to "make a life by combining what is best of the Indian way with the best of the white way." They are capable of fitting into a role made necessary by the reservation complex wherein two contrasting societies attempt to function under a common political system. They can talk to and better understand both sides. At the same time, these leaders *are Indian-oriented*. They want to be accepted by the Indian society and want to maintain Indian identity, but both the bicultural milieu and their personal qualities lead to an understanding and participation that differs from that of the chiefs.

The interpreters know much of the old religion and lore. Quite often their fathers had been of the chief class and these men had been taught some of the traditions in their homes. But they are not committed, openly at least, to the old religion. They are members, and often leaders, of Christian churches. Those who are Catholics look for elements in Catholicism that support Indian values and they are adept at finding Christian analogues for Blackfeet beliefs. Others have joined minor Protestant churches and stress that the predominant Indian attendance at these makes them Indian churches. There is some evidence that many Indian-oriented persons are changing church affiliation frequently and that this is caused possibly by a search for a white church that is most congruent with the Black-feet religion.[17]

The interpreters participate in Indian ceremonies and are given parts to play in the Sun Dance. They do not have the traditional wisdom required for the roles, but they are Indian leaders who are sympathetic and "good." They tend to express Indian values, and subscribe to Indian symbols. Interpreters frequently put up a tepee for Indian Days, wear a chiefly costume on appropriate occasions, stress their Indian names, and belong to a men's society.

In addition to their Indian training, these men have had the opportunity to get a good education in American schools, to travel and otherwise become experienced with much of white culture. They are capable of competing with the white-oriented, and through ability, hard work, and some economic success are well accepted by the white-oriented community. They could succeed on their own in any rural off-reservation community. The interpreters are not wealthy. They usually earn good salaries in agency or council positions but they use this income to help support a family ranch. Their less acculturated kinsmen work the ranch in return for some financial support. All share in the profits and losses from the enterprise.

---

[16] In an earlier paper I included the interpreters among what I called the 150% Men—people who knew two cultures well (McFee 1968).

[17] The Blackfeet have not accepted the peyote cults common to so many Indian reservations even though these are active in reservations in the surrounding region.

Because of their Indian-orientation, however, they must curb their economic ambitions in order to maintain their status. The very capabilities that make them valuable leaders within their group subject them to constant surveillance and criticism. In addition, their youth is held against them. In the past, status through wisdom came with age and in the eyes of many of their people they are wise too soon. So these men cannot acquire too much; they must be generous and helpful, and build a following that will attest to their wisdom, skill, and generosity in future years.

It is possible that in later life these men might take over the positions of custodians of tradition as these become vacated by the present chiefs, but this is doubtful, even though some people occasionally refer to them as "young chiefs." The tentative prediction would be that high status positions of both types will be filled from below where the factors of relative education and experience tend to produce differential experience within the Indian-oriented society. People of lower status already give indications as to how these positions will be filled.

The interpreters also differ from the chiefs, and many other Indian-oriented people as well, in the furnishing and maintenance of their homes. Most of the chiefs live in small frame or log houses with minimal services and simple furniture. They rarely have appliances—a wood range serves for both cooking and heating. The structures are unpainted inside and out and no attempt has been made to fence or otherwise mark the house lot or "territory." The interpreters, on the other hand, seem to have accepted more of the white-oriented interest in things. As a class, they live in larger three- or five-room houses which are painted on the inside at least. They build closets, have more furniture, own refrigerators, radios, and television sets. Often there is a fenced area around the house or some other border defining feature. The interpreters' homes look like those of many middle status white-oriented families—larger and better furnished than that of Bob Sorrel Horse, but not as freshly painted and filled with things as was Ray Hawkins' home. Here again is a sign that the interpreters aim for the best of two worlds.

INDIAN-ORIENTED LOW STATUS Low status Indian-oriented people can be described by characteristics quite similar to those of the same status in white-oriented society. These people are poor. Some are hard workers and others improvident, but lack of training limits these men to irregular wage labor. They do not find regular seasonal jobs but must take work where and when they can find it. Several of the improvident ones, like their white-oriented counterparts, are called "bums" and "winos" and are problem cases for the authorities. But there is a difference between men of the differing orientations even at the lowest status level. They face in different cultural directions, and the analysis of the data from my sample showed that the Indian-oriented low status man is more a part of his society than the lower-class white man is in his.

In contrast with the white-oriented group, economic factors fail to separate the low from many of the middle status people in Indian-oriented society. Irregular work, low income, poorly maintained and crowded houses are characteristics shared by people variously ranked on the status scale. The ultimate criterion for status assignment is social participation.

Low status people do not take part in as many social activities as do the people of higher positions; they are often present but usually as onlookers. It is significant, however, that they are not isolated from their group as is often the case with the improvident white-oriented person. The low status Indian-oriented man is welcome to attend Indian activities if he behaves. If he misbehaves he is eased out, perhaps locked up in the jail, but people do not disown him for this. They joke about it as if his actions were to be expected, and welcome him back when he settles down. If he behaves he may be given a job to do, such as ushering, police duty, or helping with the serving of the food. He is one of them, perhaps a kinsman, at least a familiar person in the community and he is given some community support.

These men have much spare time and spend a great deal of it in the street corner groups. If they, or one of their friends, have a little cash or can beg some from a tourist, they will buy a bottle of wine and get drunk. Such loafing and drinking groups are made up of Indian-oriented people.

These men fill a traditional and expected status. The Blackfeet had, in the past, a few improvident and unfortunate people who lacked the "power" to succeed. This was not held against them and it was a social duty to see that they did not starve. The low status people of today are treated in much the same way; they are thought of as unlucky and not entirely responsible for their condition. They may stir up trouble but the tendency is to keep the quarrels within the group; they are criticized and admonished but not ostracized. White and white-oriented persons let the more impersonal authorities deal with the low status trouble makers and expect public agencies to take care of the shiftless ones. The Indian-oriented group feels a responsibility for their own low status people. They are "our people" and "we"' take care of them. Family and group responsibility does not end when authorities step in, and the improvident are cared for regardless of welfare. The aid may be given grudgingly but it is forthcoming.

INDIAN-ORIENTED MIDDLE STATUS   The majority of the Indian-oriented group are assigned to a middle status that encompasses a broad range of individual differences. The same qualities requisite for high status count here, and conformity to Indian values is more important than economic condition.

These are the people who live the Indian-oriented life described in the previous chapters, who affirm the Indian-oriented values and both support and take part in the Indian-oriented society. The middle class actively supports the leaders of their choice in both the traditional and the modern spheres and differs from the lower status people because of their more complete involvement in the life of the community. It is the attitudes, opinions, acts, and wants of these people that assign and validate social status; they are the Indian-oriented public that awards some people with loyalty and influence and penalize others with gossip, criticism, and shame.

This class includes people with a wide range of knowledge of and skills in the traditional culture, and in education and experience with the white. These differences in their knowledge and skills establish both limitations on and possibilities for upward mobility for these people. The poorly educated person cannot expect to gain high status of the interpreter type, and as a consequence they are most apt to follow the pattern established by the chiefs. There is evidence in the behavior of several men that they have such ambitions. They have quit drinking and "chasing around," and have become active in a men's society, a dancing or singing group, and are learning more of the old culture from association with the chiefs. They serve on committees that plan and stage the Indian Days celebration and holiday dances, and attempt to live up to the highest values of the group. Their families are supporting them in this move. The brother of one such man spoke of him proudly: "My brother quit drinking twenty years ago and learned Indian singing. He won a singing contest and now he's a champion singer. He's the boss." Others support the similar ambitions of one of their relatives; they say that this man "isn't so much of a singer" and that he really "doesn't know much" about Blackfeet ways. His ambitions are being challenged as a part of the validation process he must go through.

Several younger men appear to be grooming for the interpreter high status positions. They are learning Blackfeet traditions in their homes or from the elders, and at the same time are doing well in school. One man appears to be a likely candidate for a position as an interpreter. He went on to college and gained additional experience in American society; he is fluent in both languages and was raised and trained in aspects of the old culture. His Indian-oriented accomplishments and success in school already have gained him the respect of the Indian-oriented, and his early success in school earned the respect of many in the white and white-oriented community. He is now going through another testing, having dropped out of college and returned to the reservation to pick up irregular labor and drinking patterns that are not appreciated by the higher status people of either orientation. Nonetheless he is forgiven by the Indian-oriented and will be by the white-oriented if he "straightens out" later and picks up his previous goals of assuming the interpreter role. Other interpreters have traveled this road.

I visited many kinds of Indian-oriented homes and with the exception of those of the interpreters found one characteristic common to all—regardless of the size of the house or financial standing of the owner, they gave little evidence of concern for the material possessions prized by middle-class whites. For instance, one middle status Indian-oriented family, the Chief Sons, lived in a four room frame house in Browning. The siding of the thirty year old structure had been covered during the past ten years with asphalt shingles; the shingle roof was in good repair, but the outside trim had not been painted since the original application. The floors were covered with linoleum, the plastered interior walls retained the original paint. The plumbing fixtures had been installed or replaced in 1958 and were in good repair. Heat was provided by the wood range. Each bedroom had a bed, a wooden chair, and a small table. Clothes were hung on wall hooks and on a cord stretched across one corner of the room. The living room was furnished with a worn davenport, a table and some wooden chairs, and an old cabinet phonograph and radio combination that was inoperative. Floral print paper curtains hung at the windows, several Russell prints and a religious calendar were on the walls, and a plaster religious figurine stood on the radio cabinet. Family photographs, including many of the children, and elders too, in Indian costumes were displayed in the bedrooms. It appeared that meals were eaten at a small table in the kitchen. Inside everything was worn, orderly, and clean; outside there was less order. There was no fence, no lawn, and several shrubs grew unattended. There was little to indicate any concern about how the place looked to a passerby.

Another Indian-oriented middle status home was an old log cabin to which an entryway and bedroom had been added. The structure was sound but unpainted. The old cabin part served as a combination kitchen, living room, and bedroom. There was no water service. Water had to be carried daily from a community hydrant a block away in three water buckets that were placed on a bench beside the wood range and a washstand. The range did double duty for cooking and heating. The furniture consisted of a plain wooden table and wooden kitchen chairs and the beds—two in the bedroom and one in the main room. As in the first house, clothes were hung on wall hooks. There were cotton print curtains at the windows and colorful patchwork quilts covered the beds. The walls were covered with family photographs, a religious calendar, and some articles of Indian beadwork. Paper flowers were on the table, and several plants were growing in tin cans that had been covered with colored paper and placed along the window sill in the entryway. Again, everything inside was neat and clean contrasting with the unfenced yard which was bare of plantings and cluttered with debris.

These examples support but do not prove my impression that there is a difference between the two orientation groups in the way they furnish and maintain their homes. I was in several middle status homes that, like the first one I described, had a refrigerator and overstuffed furniture and that, with the exception of the interpreters' homes, came closest to "having everything," as one of the Chief Sons family said of their house. Cleanliness and decoration with things that interested the family were important, but no one seemed to feel that paint was required. Exteriors received only the most necessary repairs, and the Indian-oriented more often than not showed little concern about marking off or maintaining a private space around the house. Thus there was attention to comfort, but it did not seem to be the same kind of material comfort sought by the middle-class whites.

White and white-oriented people seemed to want to define their yards and order them, which may be in part an expression of concern about what others might think: lawns, fences, flowers, and paint are status symbols in white middle-class society, but have little part to play in establishing a social position among the Indian-oriented. The latter are interested in doing other things with their time and money.

These differences remain impressionistic and need further and careful study. The new housing, freshly painted, that has indoor plumbing, hot and cold running water, electric or gas ranges, space heaters, and that encourages the building of fences and the planting of lawns will both encourage their use and maintenance and provide a test for my thesis that the two groups differ in their evaluation of such things. Time will tell how much the Indian-oriented people choose to invest in these, and whether or not they will differ from their white-oriented neighbors in this respect. For the present, at least, I find these differing concerns about work, money, home furnishings and maintenance, generosity and proper social relationships, and the values that underlie them, to be basic to the maintenance of the contrasting social structures of the two groups.

9

The Future

Summation

THIS STUDY OF THE MODERN BLACKFEET has provided evidence that the tribe is made up of two contrasting societies, each with its own culture, associational patterns and internal organization. These contrasting societies are held together because all tribal members are "Indians" by both legal and social definitions, and because they live together on an Indian reservation. The two societies also participate in economic and political systems at the tribal level that are held in common, and these systems, in turn, are intricately involved in the economic and political life of the State of Montana and therefore the nation. In addition, various kinds of kinship ties, coincident interests and associations form weaker bonds between the groups. Most of the arguments in support of this conclusion have been set forth, so only the salient characteristics of the two societies will be summarized as a basis for some reflections about the future of the Blackfeet tribe.

White-Oriented Society

The white-oriented society was found to be organized around basic values of work, self-dependence, individuality, and acquisitiveness. People of this orientation believe in these values and, in general, practice them. They keep busy, hold steady jobs, stress their ability to take care of themselves, and rarely turn to people outside their immediate family for help.

White-oriented persons work toward future goals. They want to build toward the social and economic betterment of themselves and their children and believe that this can be accomplished best by education, hard work, and acquisitiveness. To this end they build ranches, farms, or businesses, or hold a good steady job. Acquisitiveness is evidenced in the ownership and maintenance of property, homes, furnishings, and equipment that contribute to economic independence, material comfort, and serve also to symbolize, both to the individual and others, the degree of success achieved.

Persons of this orientation associate mainly with people of similar orientation and aspire toward full participation in white society. Such aspirations often are thwarted both because white people identify the white-oriented with an Indian stereotype, and they too see themselves as "Indians" in opposition to "white men" when the privileges of Indian status are under attack. The aspirations are realistic, however, because in most respects the white-oriented segment of the Blackfeet tribe differs little from the majority section of American society.

A brief investigation of the status system within this group revealed a pattern similar to the general American class structure. Like most other Americans, white-oriented people make their judgments of individual worth according to standards introduced and maintained by the dominant society. One can conclude that the white-oriented society among the Blackfeet is organized around a series of class norms. An individual who aspires to belong to this society will find social support to the extent that he approximates the behavior set by these norms and displays a commitment to the values of the group.

Indian-Oriented Society

The patterns of the Indian-oriented group stand out clearly despite the many features shared with both white and white-oriented society, and especially in the areas of contrasting premises and values. The major goal of this group is to retain its ethnic identity as shown by the attachment these people have to things and practices that symbolize Indian-ness. Traditional definitions of the good person, and particularly the value placed upon generosity, persist and serve as both symbols of being Indian, and a check against the achievement necessary for full economic integration with the dominant society.

This goal tends to make the Indian-oriented Blackfeet present rather than future oriented. They asserted tradition, a tradition made up of remembered Blackfeet culture, borrowed pan-Indian elements and incorporated elements from white culture, but this is not to be interpreted as living in the past. The future is uncertain for most Indian-oriented people; past experience has made them suspicious of long range plans. Consequently the tendency is to avoid risking present positions for unknown future benefits, to live each day as it comes and to remember real and legendary better days of the past.

The Blackfeet Indian-oriented society is organized in conformity to these norms and expectations. A man is judged by his display of Indian traits and particularly by how generous he is with the fruits of his achievement. Expressions of such judgments were recorded and used to construct a scale of status, from low to high, and the resulting class structure appeared little related to similar levels in both the general American society and the white-oriented Blackfeet group.

Of particular importance, as an indication of Indian-oriented accommodation to the bicultural milieu, is the duality apparent in the Indian system that led to the identification of two high status classes—the chiefs and the interpreters. The chiefs attain influence because of their knowledge of the past; they represent continuity with the Blackfeet forebears and the traditional culture. The interpreters, on the other hand, are supported because of their knowledge of and experience with both cultures which enables them to mediate between the subordinate and dominant groups.

The Indian-oriented society in these ways provides tribal members with an alternative route to influence and higher status—another set of class norms regulating the behavior of persons who wish to associate with people who aspire to be Indians. Approximation of these norms and evidence of commitment to the values of the group will help a man gain acceptance and social support from this society.

Two hundred and thirty years of adaptation and adjustment to change has resulted in a bicultural community held together by special bonds. The past events have not resulted in tribal disorganization, but in a reorganization that accommodates the simultaneous persistence of many traditional social and cultural characteristics from both interacting societies. A large part of the tribe has adopted the culture of the dominant society and aspires to assimilate. A smaller number, for reasons already mentioned, retains more from the Blackfeet past and resists further change. The reservation social structure has changed to accommodate these contrasting points of view. The structure of a nonreservation community tends to be unilinear, with one general set of values, and one status hierarchy. But the physical and social boundaries of the reservation and the tribe incorporate two societies, and make possible a bilinear structure that offers a choice of alternative limitations and possibilities for adaptation. An individual, consciously or otherwise, can choose, and possibly choose again, which pattern he wishes to follow. His choice, and his acceptance and class assignment, depend upon what he brings to the situation in the way of aspirations, experiences, and capabilities. Herein may lie the potential for the development of a true and viable cultural pluralism that can serve as a model for American society as a whole. That hope guides my reflections upon the future.

What Lies Ahead for the Blackfeet?

An oracle, whether a social scientist or anything else short of Delphian, takes risks. I put myself in double jeopardy: my reading of the present may be faulty, and, as is most usual, the future conditions may be very different from those I foresee.

No one in the present day should be unaware of the problems confronting American Indians, and what I have described should indicate that the Blackfeet too have troubles. There is heavy drinking, even alcoholism, among too many old and young alike. Crime, vandalism, and juvenile delinquency are too frequent. Several cases of suicide have been reported; alcohol-related and tragic deaths from violence, automobile accidents, and exposure too often occur. Underlying all this is the pervasive poverty and lack of economic opportunity that undermines self-esteem.

Too often, I think, these problems have been described as Indian problems, when they are mostly local expressions of national problems. Such an emphasis has tended to reinforce a negative stereotype of the Indian held by many neighboring whites and even by some of the white-oriented tribal members. The Indian aspect of these problems is that the Indian-oriented tend to be treated as second-class citizens on the reservation, and they, and the white-oriented as well, are treated as second-class citizens off the reservation. This creates resentment for all and identity problems for many of the young people. Some of the resulting frustrations are expressed in ways that create social problems. Beyond this, the causal factors and their antisocial expression are the same as those to be found in every community in the country, and like most other communities, the Blackfeet recognized the problems and are trying to do something about them. A Crisis Clinic, Alcoholics Anonymous, Community Action Programs, the town, the tribe, the B.I.A., church and civic organizations, and concerned citizens are at work. The solutions to these problems may be found elsewhere, they may be found here. Information, support and sympathy are needed: sensational publicity is rightfully resented.

These and other problems should not be glossed over or ignored, but at the same time they should not be stressed to the neglect of more positive aspects. The positive side to the problems described above is that they are recognized by local people and that local people are trying to do something about them. Prophets of gloom and doom are not hard to find, so in these final pages I am going to look more at the strengths than at the weaknesses to show some of the things that I think augur a better future for the Blackfeet.

The problems of an inadequate economic base and the attendant poverty are all pervasive, but these too have been recognized for a long time and the tribe, bureau, and town of Browning have been cooperating in attempts to create a viable economy. History militates against predictions of success in these endeavors. It is easy to see in retrospect how planners erred when they began so early and persisted so long in promoting small subsistence farming and ranching as the key to Indian economic security, at a time when the trend in these occupations was toward increased use of machinery and the utilization of increasingly larger land holdings. Present plans, too, may prove to be out of step with future trends. These trends, of course, are difficult to identify and action to improve the economy must be taken on the basis of the best predictions and the hope that some of the plans will be in tune with tomorrow.

The present plans for reservation economic development are predicated on (1) relocation of some of the population to industrial centers through federal support for on the job training, (2) attracting small industries and their payrolls to the reservation, and (3) increased exploitation of tourism. Success depends not only on how well these are implemented, but on where they lead.

Of these ventures, I am least optimistic about the relocation programs. These were not discussed in earlier chapters because my major concern was with events on the reservation and because accurate figures about the results of the past years efforts are not available. Bureau reports show upwards of sixty persons per year off the reservation engaged in on-the-job training or in vocational schools, but I do not know the actual rate of permanent relocation. I have talked to several men, and have heard of others, who tried relocation and for varying reasons failed and came back home. I have been told that many of those who are reported to have made a success of these ventures were already off reservation and employed prior to their entering the program. These men had availed themselves of the opportunity to better their job. These programs affect the reservation economy, however, by reducing the level of unemployment on the reservation and by contributing to the training of those who leave and return. There has been gain for individuals, but to my mind, the gain to the reservation has been slight. Too few have successfully relocated to have reduced significantly the number of unemployed, and the skills learned by those who have gone to the cities and returned more often than not have been of little use on the reservation.

I would question, too, the compatibility of this program with present trends in the cities. Relocation is being supported at a time when our cities are becoming increasingly untenable, fraught with the problems of underemployment, decaying housing, underfinanced services and overtaxed transportation facilities. It does not seem to be the proper time to encourage Indians to go to the city where they must learn and try to hold a job in a situation of possibly declining employment, and risk as well the possibility of having to move into the local poverty pockets of wretched housing. I would think that one would choose poverty among friends and in the country over poverty in the city among strangers. I feel that relocation programs are dead end streets that might be opened if they were redirected toward providing employment for Indians in small industries in small cities, at least until we can read with more certainty what the future holds for our major cities.

If it develops that the solution to city problems results in further decentralization of industry and population, then the present plans for local industrial development may turn out to be the plans of farsighted men. At present the reservation seems too far from population and commercial centers to attract industry, but it is on main transportation routes and has space, clean air, clean water and a good supply of capable, if untrained, workers. These features could be very attractive to management personnel who like the country, the scenery, hunting, fishing, and outdoor sports and are disenchanted with the city and its problems. But, if industry does come, the planning must be such that these advantages are preserved and some of the benefits of that industry accrue to the present residents. Industry will have to be more conservative and less exploitive of the natural and human resources of the region than it has been elsewhere.

The tribe and the townspeople have made a heavy investment and have incurred a considerable debt to build the Industrial Park, to make the sewer, water, and street improvements, to build homes in preparation for industrial expansion, and to make the community attractive to management personnel. If things work out, these debts will be self-liquidating and the reservation community will have made marked economic progress. If the industries do not come, things will be no worse than before. The physical improvements will remain, and better housing was sorely needed. True, everybody will be deeper in debt, but debts have been incurred for less important reasons. Capable administrators in many other U.S. towns have elected the same route to the revival of local economies.

An extension of the recent and steady upward trend in tourist activity supports a prediction of success for this venture. Again space, water, clean air, in addition to good hunting and fishing and the proximity to Glacier National Park, provide a strong base for tourist development. Tourist facilities appear to be a sound investment that would, in the long run, continue to bring in outside money regardless of the ups and downs of the national economy. The trends in this industry can be influenced by what developments take place in the cities. Will changes encourage city dwellers to spend more of their leisure time at home, or result in ever increasing search for open space and sport? Concerns for the environment will play a part in the planning and building of tourist facilities. What if studies show that tourist activities should be curtailed in the interest of preserving the very attractions the local people wish to exploit? What is the future for the automobile, motorboating, motorcycles, and ski-mobiles? Substitutes for the internal combustion engine will change the nature of motor service operations. Radical changes in recreational facilities might result, if automobile and related private, engine-powered personal transportation and sports equipment were curtailed and mass public transport was expanded. Highway construction, parking facilities, power boat and automobile servicing facilities, motels, campgrounds designed for auto traffic all would be affected. Different kinds of facilities would be needed depending on the forms of transportation that evolved. Curtailment of motor driven equipment might greatly increase the use of horses for recreation. The reservation is well suited for raising horses, and already has more than are needed for present purposes. A right guess here would make a big difference in the odds for success in tourist development. The positive aspect here is that the resources are on or near the reservation and at present these are relatively untouched. There is less of a vested interest to oppose change than would be the case if the region had already been highly developed. Little present or planned development would stand in the way of such a change.

Another trend that some predict for the U.S. economy that may affect the outcome of reservation programs is the prospect that computers and other forms of mechanization will put work as we know it out of style. If, in the next few decades, there will be fewer jobs as we know them one of two things will have to happen. The high value placed on work for its own sake will have to give way to other measures of personal worth, or other activities now called play or recreation will have to be brought into the definition of work. In either case such a change would seem to work against the success of the industrial development, but boost the prospects of success in the area of recreation. Many tribal members who have trouble finding jobs, but have developed the skills of crafts, art, and sociability may find themselves better prepared for the future than those who appear successful under present conditions. Projected plans for some form of minimum guaranteed income would have unforeseen results but could be only an improvement over present conditions.

Local and tribal participation in these attempts at solving the economic problems of the reservation have contributed along with many other experiences to the development of an increasingly viable and capable group of community leaders. This is my greatest source of optimism. The Blackfeet have never lacked for active and intelligent leaders and they have had years of experience in practical politics. The heartening factor has been the trend to a broader political base, increased autonomy of decision, and the greater participation by more of the community in political and social action. With each passing generation those who have taken leadership roles have had more education and more experience with the outside world than those who preceded them. Tribal members play leading roles in national Indian organizations. They have in the past and continue to serve in the state legislature and senate. There were Blackfeet at Alcatraz. More youth are going to college and some of these are talking of returning to the reservation to play a part in solving local problems. The tribal council and its committees has always provided a good training ground for leadership. To this has been added the Community Action Programs and other O.E.O. sponsored activities. The Browning Industrial Development Corporation and the Housing Authority, both provide opportunities for leadership training and participation for more people. Some of the O.E.O. programs are reminiscent of the old C.C.C. programs that provided short range income that was a help for people when they needed it, but had few long range economic benefits. The Community Action Programs, however, appeal to me most because they are involving young and old and most of them are centered in the community. The workers involved get to know their neighbors, learn of the community problems and what resources are available to help solve them. Even youngsters out cleaning up vacant lots are doing something with their neighbors for the community. They are learning about organization and practical politics—knowledge that should stand them in good stead whatever the future brings. The faults of these programs and organizations are the faults of all of us, as are the strengths. The Blackfeet are becoming increasingly able to run their own affairs with less governmental paternalism.

That last sentence raises the very sensitive issue of termination. This is a very sticky problem, too complicated to elaborate on here. I will side with those who oppose it for the following reasons. I agree with those tribal members who fear political domination by the county and state if the Bureau of Indian Affairs and the special relationships between tribe and the federal government were terminated. First, land would be lost rapidly if trust restrictions were removed. It is of course every citizen's right to buy and sell his property, but too many Indian owners still are too inexperienced in financial matters to protect their own interests in even the most honest land transactions or to benefit by converting land to cash. Secondly, much reservation land would be lost if it was removed from trust status and put on the tax rolls at a time when too few Indian owners make enough money from their land to meet taxes. Thirdly, the Indians feel that the present climate of discrimination in off-reservation communities would result in loss of services, poorer services, and unfair treatment in local and state courts is present federal and tribal programs were turned over to county and state. I think their fears are well founded.

The other side of the argument has some merit too. B.I.A. programs have often been overprotective, fostering overdependency and expectations of paternalistic care and these have created some problems. Some of the hamlets, particularly Heart Butte, are so dependent on tribal and governmental help that the people could not exist there without it. One result of termination would be that the people in Heart Butte would lose their remaining lands and be forced to move. This move would take them into slum areas of Browning or Great Falls, and fully on the welfare rolls of those communities. The new economic base must be secured before the trust protection can be removed.

The Blackfeet complain about the bureau but fear the alternatives more. Some of their leaders think the best move would be to let Indians assume administrative positions in the bureau where they could have more say about what should be done and how to do it. This, they say, "would hold the wolves at bay, while we work out our problems."

Termination is just one more product of the red man's burden—the white man problem. Not only have the white men taken over most of the land, the authority, and decision making powers about Blackfeet life, liberty, and pursuit of happiness, but they have married into the tribe as well. All these influences have produced, among other things, white-oriented tribal members. White people remain a problem on the reservation, some more of a problem than others. The white merchants, ranchers, and farmers, at least, are known; some are good friends. Their roles are familiar and for better or for worse predictable patterns of interaction have been established. White Bureau of Indian Affairs employees usually fit into known patterns too. Their roles are known and people recognize that some will visit with them, become friends and help out in community affairs, while others will remain aloof. Public Health Service employees are less well known. Most, with a few appreciated exceptions, come and go more frequently than do the bureau employees. They tend to remain isolated in their own residential area, and rarely enter into the economic and social life of the community.

It has been my experience that white people living around the reservation tend to be more hostile to the Blackfeet than those who live further away. The Blackfeet know, and often dislike, the established relationships in the neighboring off reservation towns. These feelings are unfortunate. People of very similar backgrounds and interests are prevented from establishing what could be very congenial friendships if these attitudes did not prevail. More Blackfeet would find off reservation jobs available if their white neighbors could exercise their biases more selectively. White-oriented tribal members, too, often lose touch with the Indian-oriented, stereotype them and, as a consequence, are branded in return with the white man stereotype.

Then there is the white tourist: a whole industry is being planned to attract greater numbers of them and their money to the reservation, yet all tourists are not loved. Too many American tourists do not know what to expect of Indians, or arrive with wrong expectations so firmly fixed that they cannot learn from experience. Too many look for the movie or comic strip Indian, the "noble red man" in buckskins or feathers who says "How" and talks about "bucks" and "squaws" and "papooses," and is considered to be either inordinately wise and taciturn or somewhat short on intelligence. Others seem to expect to find illiterate people living in squalor and filth. They may find some of what they expect. Some Indians dress up for them and play the movie Indian for the edification of the tourist and the benefit of their own pocketbooks. Visitors can see a drunken Indian, there is poverty, unkempt appearing housing, and not everything is neat and orderly in appearance. But they have excluded the large and significant middle: the educated and industrious who are all around them wherever they go. They have not entered the houses that appear as shacks on the outside, but are clean, orderly homes inside. They have excluded the many who are impoverished but not licked. All of these are hurt when people, who must think that none of them can understand English, make audible derogatory remarks about them, their homes, their town, and their children. The Blackfeet do not talk of "bucks, squaws, and papooses," and feel that these terms indicate that they are less than human. They are men and women, have husbands, wives, and children, like anybody else. They react with concealed resentment, and usually with extraordinary courtesy, when someone enters a restaurant and then leaves, saying loudly: "Let's go somewhere else. This is run by Indians and is apt to be dirty." The charitable ones chalk such behavior up to ignorance on the part of that tourist; it is that, but it is bad manners as well. Luckily not all white tourists, just too many of them, are like that. It is part of the Indian's white man problem.

Among other white visitors to the reservation is the anthropologist. I have a vested interest, a bias here, that must be recognized, so will not examine this problem in all its detail. I only offer a few defenses: anthropologists have recorded much of what Blackfeet elders told them of the past culture, and modern Indians do turn to these records to learn of their past and use these books as guides for the revival and perpetuation of tradition. For my part, I can only hope that I have repaid some of my debt to the Blackfeet by not acting like the worst of the tourists, and that by this book and my teaching I can educate future tourists not only to better behavior, but more importantly to a greater appreciation for and understanding of the Blackfeet in all their variety.

There is one more development that bolsters my optimism: That which I will call the third generation phenomenon. The children of white-oriented families who have achieved a measure of economic security are taking an increased interest in Indian traditions. They are buying or making costumes, learning to dance and participating in the Indian Days and community social events. As some say, "They are taking an interest in their Indian heritage." This is being furthered too, by the college youth who have been taken up in the red power and other student Indian movements. They and their peers on the reservation are not only asserting their Indian identity, but their tribal identity as well. Over the past decade I have noticed not only the more recent participation of the third generation white-oriented, but the earlier shift from costume, song, and dance that was Indian, to a greater emphasis on those things that are authentically Blackfeet Indian.

These young people can play an important part in the elimination of white-oriented misunderstanding of and unrecognized discrimination against the Indian-oriented. They can be interpreters from the white-oriented side who can work with the Indian-oriented interpreters toward better understanding and cooperation between the two social divisions of the Blackfeet community. In the best of all worlds such communication could lead to a unified but diverse community, a working cultural pluralism, a more viable society that could solve its own problems and deal with and eliminate most of its white man problems. Utopian? Perhaps. But I think that the seeds of such a development are present and that the maintenance of the reservation system for a while longer might allow it to work out.

Credit too must be given to the Indian-oriented and the full-bloods, past and present, who have endured, who have persisted in preserving what they cherished and believed in in the face of strong and often violent opposition. They have maintained traditions. These traditions have posed a dilemma for some who find it difficult to choose between the old and the new, but have given many others a source of identity and pride that has enriched the quality of reservation life.

Epilogue

Albert Buffalo Heart and most of his peers have died during the past decade. Some of their names, along with those of deceased white-oriented tribal leaders, can be read on a plaque at the entrance to the Museum of the Plains Indian. He and men like him have left a legacy of past tradition—knowledge and beliefs, modified by their personal interpretations and understandings. Some of their medicine bundles and other possessions symbolic of their power, experiences, and continuity with preceding generations have gone into museum and private collections. Others have been transferred to members of their families or other tribal members who may or may not perpetuate the beliefs and activities that went with the symbols.

A new generation of elders has taken their place and these will play the role in different ways and from slightly different backgrounds. Some of the new chiefs own bundles, know some rituals and parts of others. Some of them do not. They all share a knowledge of the language and a commitment to perpetuating the traditions as they know them. What they know and do will undoubtedly be reformulated by them into a fairly cohesive and organized Blackfeet "tradition," somewhat different from that which went before, but still capable of providing support for a continuing Indian-orientation. Young men are preparing to fill these roles in their own turn.

John Arrowhead is still there. His life goes on with little noticeable change from year to year. Roy Conrad is dead and his sons carry on the farm and too, perhaps, the memories of what their father told them of his life, his knowledge and experiences. Bob Sorrel Horse still works but falls short of his dream. In fact much changes and much remains the same.

Amid the ebb and flow, the change and the sameness, in spite of the continuing tragic waste of talent and potential, a younger generation is developing that should be better able to meld the old and the new. The future reservation citizens should be better able to mediate the social divisions and to work toward producing a viable cultural pluralism. Hopefully, the Raymond Black Plumes and the Henry Rogers will come closer together in understanding and in their aspirations, and teach their children to incorporate the legacy of their parents, the teachings of the school, and what they learn by participation in reservation life into their own tradition—a tradition that does include, or allow expression of, the best of the Indian way and the best of the white. If diversity is as important to the perpetuation of a people and a culture as it is for the survival of a biological species, then the future generations of the Blackfeet have been well served by the diversity bequeathed them by their ancestors.

References

BLACKFEET INDIAN RESERVATION, TOWN OF BROWNING, 1968, "Model City" Application. (Mimeographed) Browning, Montana.

BLACKFEET TRIBAL COUNCIL, n.d., Records and Documents. Browning, Montana.

BRADLEY, LT. JAMES H., 1900, "Affairs at Fort Benton," *Contributions to the Historical Society of Montana* 3:201–287.

———, 1923, "St. Peter's Mission," *Contributions to the Historical Society of Montana* 9:315–316.

BROPHY, WILLIAM A., and SOPHIE D. ABERLE, 1966, *The Indian: America's Unfinished Business.* Norman, Oklahoma: University of Oklahoma Press.

BRUNER, EDWARD M., 1956, "Primary Group Experience and the Processes of Acculturation," *American Anthropologist* 58:605–623.

BURLINGAME, MERRILL, G., 1942, *The Montana Frontier.* Helena, Montana: State Publishing Company.

EWERS, JOHN C., 1955, "The Horse in Blackfoot Indian Culture," Bureau of American Ethnology, *Bulletin 159.*

———, 1958, *The Blackfeet: Raiders on the Northwestern Plains.* Norman, Oklahoma: University of Oklahoma Press.

FAGG, HARRISON G., and ASSOCIATES, 1970, *Browning-Blackfeet Comprehensive Plan.* Billings, Montana.

The Glacier Reporter (Browning, Montana), 1959–1970.

GLOVER, RICHARD, 1962, *David Thompson's Narrative: 1784–1812.* Toronto: The Champlain Society.

GRINNELL, GEORGE BIRD, 1907, *Blackfoot Lodge Tales.* New York: Charles Scribner's Sons.

KAPPLER, CHARLES J., 1903, See U.S. Congress, Senate.

LEWIS, OSCAR, 1942, *The Effects of White Contact Upon Blackfoot Culture with Special Reference to the Role of the Fur Trade.* Monographs of the American Ethnological Society, No. 6. Seattle: University of Washington Press.

LINTON, RALPH, 1936, *The Study of Man.* New York: Appleton-Century-Crofts, Inc.

MCCLINTOCK, WALTER, 1910, *The Old North Trail.* London: Macmillan and Co., Ltd.

MCFEE, MALCOLM, 1962, *Modern Blackfeet: Contrasting Patterns of Differential Acculturation.* Unpublished Ph.D. dissertation, Department of Anthropology, Stanford University.

———, 1968, "The 150% Man, a Product of Blackfeet Acculturation," *American Anthropologist* 70:1096–1103.

MERIAM, LEWIS, *et al.,* 1928, *The Problem of Indian Administration.* Institute for Government Research, Studies in Administration. Baltimore: The Johns Hopkins Press.

The Montana Almanac, 1957. Missoula, Montana: Montana State University Press.

ROBBINS, LYNN A., 1968, "Economics, Household Composition and the Family Cycle: The Blackfeet Case," in *Spanish-Speaking People in the United States.* Proceedings of the 1968 Annual Spring Meeting of the American Ethnological Society. Seattle: University of Washington Press.

STERN, THEODORE, 1966, *The Klamath Tribe: A People and Their Reservation*. Seattle: University of Washington Press.

TOOLE, ROSS K., 1959, *Montana: An Uncommon Land*. Norman, Oklahoma: University of Oklahoma Press.

U.S. BOARD OF INDIAN COMMISSIONERS, 1905–1925, *Annual Reports*.

U.S. CONGRESS, 1881, *Congressional Record*. Vol. XI.

————, 1886, *Congressional Record*. Vol. XVII.

————, 1953, *Congressional Record*. Vol. XCIX.

U.S. CONGRESS, SENATE, 1903, *Indian Affairs, Laws and Treaties*. Charles J. Kappler, ed. Senate Document 452, 57th Congress, 1st Session.

————, 1918, *Blackfeet Indian Reservation*. Committee on Indian Affairs, Report No. 451, 65th Congress, 2nd Session.

U.S. DEPARTMENT OF THE INTERIOR, 1934–1959, *Annual Reports of the Secretary of the Interior*.

U.S. DEPARTMENT OF THE INTERIOR, Office of Indian Affairs, 1883–1926, *Annual Reports of the Commissioner of Indian Affairs*.

————, 1936, *Constitution and By-Laws for the Blackfeet Tribe of the Blackfeet Indian Reservation, Montana*.

————, 1936, *Corporate Charter of the Blackfeet Tribe of the Blackfeet Indian Reservation, Montana*.

————, 1936, *Indians at Work*. Vol. III, No. 12; Vol. IV, No. 4; Vol. IV, No. 7; Vol. IV, No. 8.

————, 1939, *Statistical Report of Public Assistance to Indians Under the Social Security Act as of October 1, 1939*.

————, 1940, *Statistical Supplement to the Annual Report of the Commissioner of Indian Affairs, 1940*.

————, 1970, *Blackfeet Agency FY 1972 Budget and Program Memorandum*.

U.S. DEPARTMENT OF THE INTERIOR, Office of the Solicitor, 1958, *Federal Indian Law*.

U.S. STATUTES, 1859, *Statutes at Large*. Vol. XI.

————, 1875, *Statutes at Large*. Vol. XVIII.

————, 1887, *Statutes at Large*. Vol. XXIV.

————, 1889, *Statutes at Large*, Vol. XXV.

————, 1897, *Statutes at Large*. Vol. XXIX.

————, 1907, *Statutes at Large*. Vol. XXXIV.

————, 1919, *Statutes at Large*. Vol. XLI.

————, 1934, *Statutes at Large*. Vol. XLVIII.

————, 1936, *Statutes at Large*. Vol. XLIX.

————, 1950, *Statutes at Large*. Vol. LXIV, Part 1.

WEBER, KENNETH R., 1968, *Economy, Occupation, Education and Family in a Tri-Ethnic Community*. Unpublished M.A. thesis, Department of Anthropology, University of Oregon.

WHETSTONE, DANIEL W., 1956, *Frontier Editor*. New York: Hastings House Publishers, Inc.

WILLIAMS, ROBIN M. JR., 1970, *American Society: A Sociological Interpretation*. 3rd ed. New York: Alfred A. Knopf, Inc.

WILSON, H. CLYDE, 1963, "An Inquiry into the Nature of Plains Indian Cultural Development," *American Anthropologist* 65:355–369.

WISSLER, CLARK, 1910, "Material Culture of the Blackfoot Indians," *Anthropological Papers of the American Museum of Natural History* Vol. V (1).

————, 1911, "The Social Life of the Blackfoot Indians," *Anthropological Papers of the American Museum of Natural History* Vol. VII (1).

————, 1912, "Ceremonial Bundles of the Blackfoot Indians," *Anthropological Papers of the American Museum of Natural History* Vol. VII (2).

————, 1913, "Societies and Dance Associations of the Blackfoot Indians," *Anthropological Papers of the American Museum of Natural History* Vol. XI (4).

————, 1918, "The Sun Dance of the Blackfoot Indians," *Anthropological Papers of the American Museum of Natural History* Vol. XVI (3).

Recommended Reading

BROPHY, WILLIAM A., and SOPHIE D. ABERLE, 1966, *The Indian: America's Unfinished Business*. Norman, Oklahoma: University of Oklahoma Press.
The report of the Commission on the Rights, Liberties, and Responsibilities of the American Indian, authorized by the Fund for the Republic, Inc., is a good source of reliable information about the political, legal, economic, health, education, and welfare conditions of the United States Indians. Population and economic figures are already dated, and the national summaries are heavily weighted by conditions among the southwest tribes that represent a fifth of the total Indian population, so do not reflect accurately the conditions to be found in other regions. The commission assumed that the Indians should and will be assimilated and made recommendations to that end.

DOZIER, EDWARD P., 1966, *Hano: A Tewa Indian Community in Arizona*. New York: Holt, Rinehart and Winston, Inc.
A case study of the descendants of a group of Tewa-speaking Indians who left their settlement on the Rio Grande River in New Mexico at the close of the seventeenth century to establish a new village among the Hopi on First Mesa in northeastern Arizona. This is an interesting account of how these people selectively accepted and rejected aspects of Hopi life. I recommend this book because it describes a contemporary way of life, familiar to the Pueblo groups of the Southwest, but in sharp contrast to the life on the reservations of the northern and western parts of the United States.

EWERS, JOHN C., 1958, *The Blackfeet: Raiders on the Northwest Plains*. Norman, Oklahoma: University of Oklahoma Press.
Ewers has done careful research through the historical and ethnographic literature and worked, as well, with many Blackfeet informants during the years he was the curator of the Museum of the Plains Indian in Browning, Montana. This book is both a literary and professional synthesis of his research and the best single source of information about the traditional Blackfeet culture and the history of change from the buffalo days through the mid-1940s.

GRINNELL, GEORGE BIRD, 1962, *Blackfoot Lodge Tales*. Lincoln, Nebraska: University of Nebraska Press.
A paperback reissue of the 1907 publication (New York: Charles Scribner's Sons), this is a collection of Blackfeet myths and tales as told to Grinnell during his visits to the Piegan from 1885 to 1907, and includes his sympathetic, often paternalistic description of Blackfeet life and customs. A naturalist, writer, and editor and publisher of the periodical, *Forest and Stream*, Grinnell took an active part in publicizing the plight of the Indians at the turn of the century. In this book he expresses quite well the prevailing concern of the times for "civilizing" the "child-like savages." His commentary should be read with this in mind.

McCLINTOCK, WALTER, 1968, *The Old North Trail*. Lincoln, Nebraska: University of Nebraska Press.
This book, first published in 1910 (London: Macmillan and Co., Ltd.) has long

been out of print and difficult to find. McClintock first visited the Blackfeet in 1896, and spent many summers thereafter living with the Piegan along Cut Bank Creek and visiting on the Blood reserve. Here he describes the culture of the people he knew, their beliefs, customs, the ceremonies and curing rites he observed, the tepees, medicine bundles, and the things he was told about the past. This is one of the best first hand reports on the Blackfeet of that time.

NURGE, ETHEL (ed.), 1970, *The Modern Sioux: Social Systems and Reservation Culture.* Lincoln, Nebraska: University of Nebraska Press.

A collection of papers written by eleven anthropologists who have studied the contemporary Sioux. These essays provide a wealth of data, along with analytic treatment of reservation problems; the book is a forerunner of a number of similar volumes being compiled by different editors and publishers dealing with modern Indian life and problems. These and ethnographic reports on other reservation Indians in the United States will contribute much to our understanding of modern native Americans, their diversity and similarities.

SCHULTZ, J. W., 1935, *My Life as an Indian.* New York: Fawcett World Library.

This is a paperback reprint of James Willard Schultz's autobiographical novel first published in 1907. Schultz (1859–1947) came west in 1877. He settled among the Blackfeet, married a Piegan girl, and lived as a trader and rancher among the Indians for the next twenty-six years. After the death of his wife in 1903 he left the reservation and devoted much of his life to writing stories about his experiences with the Blackfeet for magazines and periodicals, such as *Boy's Life, Youths' Companion,* and Grinnell's *Forest and Stream. My Life as an Indian* was the first of several books, and gives a first hand account of the last of the buffalo days, the buffalo hide trade, the life of the white traders and their Indian wives who played an important part in the Blackfeet attempts to put together a new life after the decimation of the buffalo, and Schultz's own opinions about the events of the times.

SPINDLER, GEORGE D., and LOUISE S., 1971, *Dreamers without Power: The Menomini Indians.* New York: Holt, Rinehart and Winston, Inc.

An excellent case study of the Menomini of Wisconsin by the Spindlers who, since 1948, have studied the sociocultural and psychological adaptation of the people of this now terminated tribe. The Menomini and the Blackfeet, who speak divergent Algonkian languages and differ greatly in past cultures and their adaptations to Euro-American dominance, further illustrate the impossibility of generalizing easily about *the* American Indian.

STERN, THEODORE, 1966, *The Klamath Tribe: A People and Their Reservation.* Seattle: University of Washington Press.

This is a carefully prepared and detailed account of the Klamath of Oregon and their adaptation and adjustment to reservation life. In addition to the ethnographic and historical record, Stern gives another description of contemporary reservation life that further documents the diversity among and within Indian tribes. The Klamath were terminated in 1954 and the results of this and the Menomini termination as yet are not fully comprehended.